Making Math Accessible for the At-Risk Student

OTHER RECENTLY PUBLISHED TEACHER IDEAS PRESS TITLES

Paper Action Figures of the Imagination: Clip, Color and Create
Paula Montgomery

Fairy Tales Readers Theatre
Anthony D. Fredericks

Shakespeare Kids: Performing his Plays, Speaking his Words
Carole Cox

Family Matters: Adoption and Foster Care in Children's Literature
Ruth Lyn Meese

Solving Word Problems for Life, Grades 6–8
Melony A. Brown

Abraham Lincoln and His Era: Using the American Memory Project to Teach with Primary Sources
Bobbi Ireland

Brushing Up on Grammar: An Acts of Teaching Approach
Joyce Armstrong Carroll, EdD, HLD, and Edward E. Wilson

The Comic Book Curriculum: Using Comics to Enhance Learning and Life
James Rourke

Hello Hi-Lo: Readers Theatre Math
Jeff Sanders and Nancy I. Sanders

War Stories for Readers Theatre: World War II
Suzanne I. Barchers

Think Green, Take Action: Books and Activities for Kids
Daniel A. Kriesberg

Storytelling and QAR Strategies
Phyllis Hostmeyer and Marilyn Adele Kinsella

MAKING MATH ACCESSIBLE FOR THE AT-RISK STUDENT

GRADES 7–12

LINDA PTACEK

A TEACHER IDEAS PRESS BOOK

 LIBRARIES UNLIMITED

AN IMPRINT OF ABC-CLIO, LLC
Santa Barbara, California • Denver, Colorado • Oxford, England

Library of Congress Cataloging-in-Publication Data

Ptacek, Linda.
    Making math accessible for the at-risk student : grades 7-12 / Linda Ptacek.
        p. cm.—(A teacher ideas press book)
    Includes bibliographical references and index.
    ISBN 978-1-59884-590-7 (hard copy : alk. paper)—ISBN 978-1-59884-591-4 (ebook) 1. Mathematics—Study and teaching (Middle school) 2. Mathematics—Study and teaching (Secondary) 3. Special education—Curricula. I. Title.
    QA11.P785 2011
    510.71′2—dc22   2010041104

ISBN: 978-1-59884-590-7
EISBN: 978-1-59884-591-4

15 14 13 12 11   1 2 3 4 5

This book is also available on the World Wide Web as an eBook.
Visit www.abc-clio.com for details.

Libraries Unlimited
An Imprint of ABC-CLIO, LLC

ABC-CLIO, LLC
130 Cremona Drive, P.O. Box 1911
Santa Barbara, California 93116-1911

This book is printed on acid-free paper ∞

Manufactured in the United States of America

CONTENTS

TABLE OF ACTIVITIES

All of the activities discussed in chapters 1–6 are included as blackline masters in chapter 7. The CD that is included with this book also contains all of the activities. The following chart lists each activity's title, number, and content. The levels highlighted to the right of each title indicate whether the activity is appropriate for **P**re-Algebra, **A**lgebra, or **G**eometry. A teacher page accompanies each activity, giving special directions, teacher tips, and solutions. The teacher pages are not included on the CD.

Activity	Type	Title and Content	Levels		
1	Lesson	**Basic Geometry Terms** Student note-taking sheet	P	A	G
2	Lesson	**Characteristics of Polygons** Using examples and nonexamples to identify polygons	P	A	G
3	Game	**Cubes** A game reviewing a variety of pre-algebra topics	P	A	G
4	Game	**Cubes** A game reviewing slopes and lines	P	A	G
5	Lesson	**Defining Angles** A note-taking sheet covering nine different types of angles	P	A	G
6	Lesson	**Dog-Gone Awesome Math (DGAM)** A mnemonic device/story for solving linear equations	P	A	G
7	Lesson	**Divisibility Rules** Divisibility rules, class activity, and worksheets	P	A	G
8	Lesson	**Factoring Quadratic Trinomials: Step 1** Finding pairs of factors	P	A	G
9	Lesson	**Factoring Quadratic Trinomials: Step 2** Sums and differences of factors	P	A	G
10	Lesson	**Factoring Quadratic Trinomials: Step 3** What in the world is a quadratic trinomial?	P	A	G
11	Lesson	**Factoring Quadratic Trinomials: Step 4** Review of FOILing	P	A	G
12	Lesson	**Factoring Quadratic Trinomials: Step 5** Reading the clues and setting up the binomials	P	A	G
13	Lesson	**Factoring Quadratic Trinomials: Step 6** Putting it all together	P	A	G
14	First Week	**Alpha Math** Brainstorming math terms	P	A	G
15	First Week	**Find the Sign** Common math symbols	P	A	G
16	First Week	**Hello, My Name Is . . .** Getting-to-know-you activity	P	A	G
17	First Week	**Info Circles** Getting-to-know-you activity	P	A	G
18	First Week	**Key In to This** Calculator proficiency	P	A	G
19	First Week	**Skills Survey** Prerequisite skills assessment	P	A	G
20	Lesson	**Fraction Interaction** Comparing fractions by cross-multiplying	P	A	G
21	Lesson	**Combining Like Terms** An introduction to "like terms"	P	A	G
22	Lesson	**Greatest Common Factor, Two Methods** The double-divide method for finding the greatest common factor	P	A	G
23	Game	**Gridlock: Fractions, Decimals, and Percentages** A puzzle matching equivalent fractions, decimals, and percentages	P	A	G

Activity	Type	Title and Content	Levels		
24	Game	**Gridlock: Like Terms** Students must reassemble a puzzle by matching like terms	P	A	G
25	Game	**Gridlock: Geometry Terms** A puzzle matching geometry terms and sketches	P	A	G
26	Review	**Linear Equations 1** Counting the slope of a line	P	A	G
27	Review	**Linear Equations 2** Calculating slope given two points	P	A	G
28	Review	**Linear Equations 3** What is slope-intercept form?	P	A	G
29	Review	**Linear Equations 4** Graphing equations in slope-intercept form	P	A	G
30	Review	**Linear Equations 5** Horizontal and vertical lines	P	A	G
31	Review	**Linear Equations 6** Parallel and perpendicular lines	P	A	G
32	Song	**Number Tag: A Real Numbers Song** A song to introduce or review the real numbers	P	A	G
33	Lesson	**Mean, Median, Mode, and Range** Class activity involving data gathered from students	P	A	G
34	Lesson	**Multiplying Binomials, Check-Double-Check** Multiplying a pair of binomials using two different methods	P	A	G
35	Lesson	**Order of Operations** A pair of worksheets moving from identifying just the first step in simplifying an expression to the completion of all steps	P	A	G
36	Lesson	**Parallel Lines and Transversals** Introducing parallel lines and transversals with a limerick. Also includes four additional limericks which can be used with other math topics.	P	A	G
37	Review	**Parallel Lines, Transversals, and the Angles They Form** Comprehensive review page and worksheet	P	A	G
38	Game	**Pass It On: Plotting Ordered Pairs** A row race game about plotting ordered pairs	P	A	G
39	Game	**Pass It On: Geometric Shapes** A row race game focusing on drawing geometric figures	P	A	G
40	Lesson	**Prime Factorization, Check-Double-Check** Doing prime factorization using two different methods	P	A	G
41	Review	**Properties of Real Numbers** Introduced with numbers, variables, and real-life examples	P	A	G
42	Game	**Quads** Teams of four answer questions about linear equations	P	A	G
43	Review	**RAP (Review-and-Practice) Cards** Bulletin board idea for review-and-practice cards that students can do at the end of class if they have extra time	P	A	G
44	Lesson	**The Real Number System, No Leftovers** Real number system visual, manipulative, and song	P	A	G
45	Lesson	**Varsity Sue, a Readers Theater Play** Readers theater play and follow-up activity about circles	P	A	G

Activity	Type	Title and Content	Levels		
46	Review	**What's the Difference?** Explain the difference in pairs of pre-algebra terms	P	A	G
47	Review	**What's the Difference?** Explain the difference in pairs of algebra terms	P	A	G
48	Review	**What's Your Angle?** Interactive bulletin board focusing on angle measurement	P	A	G
49	Review	**What's Your First Step?** Identify the first step in solving a series of equations	P	A	G
50	Review	**Whatzit?** A visual with geometric figures for students to identify	P	A	G

ACKNOWLEDGMENTS

Thanks to all of my family members and friends who believed in me and who encouraged me to attack this huge project. And a special thanks to my husband, Darell, who lost me to the computer in the basement for hundreds of hours during the process of writing this book.

I'm back!

INTRODUCTION: WHY THIS BOOK?

Although I have a state teaching endorsement that labels me as "highly qualified" to teach high school mathematics, I am not a math guru. I am a special education teacher with a high school math endorsement, a very strange combination. My passion, cultivated over 35 years of teaching, is exploring seemingly complex topics and breaking them down into manageable components that at-risk students can understand. This book and the materials in it have grown from my need to keep my own teaching fresh and also to reach out to as many students as possible who are "going under."

What This Book Is Not

- It is not a textbook espousing the correct scope and sequence of topics for a secondary math class. School districts pay thousands of dollars for textbooks that do that, and yet teachers still disagree with the organization and format of these books.
- It is not a student workbook on a specific topic or a collection of blackline masters to supplement a textbook.
- It is not a formal *How to Teach Mathematics* book citing research studies and major educational theorists of the 20th century.

What This Book Is

- It is a conversationally voiced collection of materials and ideas that have worked to help at-risk students succeed in general education math classes. It is "best practices tweaked."
- It is a compilation of organizational, instructional, and motivational activities geared toward adolescents that can be used as they are presented or adapted for other content. The suggestions and activities in this book are student-friendly and age-appropriate. The wording is simple, the organization is clear, and the appearance is nonthreatening.

- It is a reminder that students have different learning styles, learning rates, and levels of frustration. Although it would be much easier for everyone involved, education is not a one-size-fits-all proposition.
- It is a challenge to teachers to think outside the box when developing lesson plans. If at first you don't succeed, try something different! Each week, choose a different technique to incorporate into your teaching. By the end of the year, not only will you have a much larger bag of tricks, but you will also have students who feel more comfortable with high school mathematics. Success is a road trip.

Who Needs This Book?

The obvious answer is *students*. Since the odds of them purchasing a math book for themselves anytime in the near future are zero, the focus groups now become the following:

- ***Special Education Teachers and Paraprofessionals:*** Special educators are frequently asked to collaborate in classrooms outside of their curricular areas. Their expertise is needed in the classroom to help with accommodations and modifications for the identified special education students. These activities can be used by special education staff for small group or individual instruction to supplement, reinforce, or reteach concepts taught in class.
- ***General Education Math Teachers:*** Teachers have seen a dramatic increase in the number of at-risk students in their classrooms over the last 10 years, yet there is still a level of uncertainty about how to best work with these students. The wide range of student abilities resulting from this increase has presented daily challenges in both classroom management and effective lesson design. The techniques and activities provided in this book can be easily incorporated into any classroom to support the math teacher in this challenging endeavor. In addition, the instructional techniques presented here reflect much of the response-to-intervention (RTI) philosophy that is being implemented nationwide in schools through the use of multitiered support systems.
- ***Librarians and Media Specialists:*** Librarians are frequently an underutilized resource for math teachers, but with their media expertise and software savvy, they can be excellent collaborative partners.
- ***Accelerated-Curriculum Teachers at the Elementary Level:*** In many districts, algebra is taught at the elementary level to select groups of students with advanced math skills. This book would be particularly helpful for those teachers because of the lessons' length and simple formatting.
- ***Student Teachers:*** Student teachers frequently are placed at different grade levels or in different subject areas than they will be teaching when they receive their first classroom assignment. The range of materials covered in this book, from pre-algebra to algebra and geometry, will be helpful to these future teachers no matter where they finally locate. The information and techniques for working with at-risk students should also help them "hit the ground running" as they start out on their teaching careers.
- ***Teachers of English Language Learners:*** Students who are new to our country, language, and culture are frequently overwhelmed in their mathematics classes because of the abstract concepts and vocabulary delivered every day. Any one piece they fail to grasp due to language or cultural differences could be that one essential building block necessary for the whole chapter. The techniques and activities in this book could be used with English language learner students to prevent this from happening.

- *Substitutes:* Many of the activities in this book can be utilized effectively by substitutes who are teaching outside of their curricular area on days when lessons run short and minutes run long.

How to Use This Book

Although this book contains activities for **pre-algebra, algebra,** and **geometry,** it has been organized with the busy teacher in mind. Throughout the first six chapters of the book, as ideas and techniques are discussed, the activities that illustrate them are noted by title in bold, underlined font followed by an activity number in parentheses, for example, **Defining Angles** (Activity 5). All activities discussed in chapters 1–6 appear as blackline masters in chapter 7. For the teacher's convenience, all of the activities are also included on the CD that accompanies this book. This will make it easier to use the materials with presentation software and also will give teachers the flexibility of using a lesson's format with other content. The types of activities included are described in the following.

- *First Week:* Activities in this category are designed to help the teacher quickly become acquainted with the students at the beginning of the year. Some are content related, and others give students an opportunity to share personal information.
- *Lessons:* These are primarily designed for introducing new material. Special formatting and framing are used to help emphasize important concepts. Some of these materials are designed specifically to help the student working significantly below grade level with note taking, basic facts, and concept retention.
- *Reviews:* These class activities and worksheets are intended to be used after the students have gained a level of mastery with the materials.
- *Songs:* These are short, curriculum-based math lyrics sung to music that students will easily recognize and be able to sing.
- *Games:* The games included in this book are ones that can be done with very little preparation on the teacher's part yet do a good job reviewing content and keeping students engaged. Instructions, game boards, questions, and solutions are provided.
- *Tools:* Several activities have accompanying "tool sheets," which are noted with a wrench symbol. See **Divisibility Rules** (Activity 7) and **Mean, Median, Mode, and Range** (Activity 33). Students should be encouraged to designate a section of their notebook as a math toolbox and to save these pages for use throughout the year.

A teacher page with special directions, tips, and solutions accompanies each of the activities. For consistent record keeping, the teacher page also contains a space to record the state or district standard(s) to which the activity correlates.
Enjoy!

Success Is a Road Trip

These days, when a family goes on a road trip, they frequently enter their destination into the GPS system mounted on their windshield and wait for instructions. One of the several voices that they can select will then guide them blissfully along their route. Life is so simple in this age of technology! In the classroom, the teacher becomes the ultimate GPS, guiding an entire roomful of young travelers on a yearlong excursion. The main goal is to have everyone arrive successfully at the destination with new math skills intact. There will be wrong turns and misunderstood directions and students who would prefer an entirely different route. The initial planning step for *your* math road trip requires a complete understanding of your destination: district objectives, state assessment indicators, and individualized education program goals for special education students in your class. Will you select the most direct route, the scenic route, or the fastest route? What will you see along the way, and how long will you spend at each stop? The answers to these questions depend to a great extent on your group of travelers. Although this book contains commonsense, best-practice teaching activities that will work for your entire class, its specific target is the student travelers who were accidentally left behind at the first rest stop!

My First Day of High School

(This was written by a ninth-grade girl. Sometimes we forget that not everyone loves school.)

Everyone was excited about their first day of high school, but not me. I was so nervous and stressed out that I could not fall asleep the night before high school began. I tried to, but I could not. So I just stared at the ceiling, wondering, thinking, and listening. I thought about my life when I was younger, and about how life was so much easier then. I thought about how much I have grown, and how 10 years seemed to last only 10 minutes. My thoughts were constantly interrupted by a voice I kept hearing, "Enjoy ninth grade now because it doesn't get any easier. It only gets harder." This did not help the anxiety I was feeling at all. I closed my eyes trying to ignore the voice echoing in my head.

The next thing I knew, Mom was banging on my door telling me it was the first day of school and to wake up. I woke up, put on clothes and my brother drove me to school. I walked through the high school doors with my head pointing to the ground, my arms folded together, and a shy look on my face. I just stood there like a statue until the bell rang to go to our first hour class.

At around fourth hour, my stress level was over the top. Although I was able to find my classes okay, there was still the matter of me being in a new school where I hardly knew any of the kids and did not know any of the teachers. All the teachers had different personalities. One was more laid back than the other one, or one accepted late work and one did not. The worst part was that I could not remember which teacher belonged to which personality. I was afraid that I was not ever going to be able to learn which teacher I could just be myself in front of and which teacher I had to keep my personality locked in a safe. I did not know anybody from first to fourth hour, so I had no one to talk to. Even with everybody in the study hall room, I felt like I was alone. I felt invisible, and like no one understood the amount of stress I was feeling. The tears that I had been fighting back since the moment I walked in the building began to stroll down my face. I wiped them away and then went up to one of the study hall teachers asking if I could go the bathroom.

I walked out trying not to let anybody see the tears that were falling from my eyes. I sagged my head, folded my arms, and walked through the hallways and down the stairs until I reached the doors leading outside. There was a corner under the stairs where I knew no one could see me crying. I curled up into a ball, and tears started coming down my face like rain falling from the sky. I wanted to be back home, where I did not feel like I was constantly being judged. I wanted to crawl under a rock until the final bell rang and school was over.

CHAPTER 1

Why Students Struggle with Math:
The Scenarios

In teacher lounges across the country, theories abound as to why students struggle in the classroom. Sometimes the finger is pointed at the student who is "lazy" or "not trying." Other times the explanation is directed at parents who lack control or a desire to be involved with their student's education. Occasionally, the teacher internalizes the blame and decides that the lesson was too difficult or was not presented well enough. None of these parties—students, parents, or teachers—ever wakes up in the morning thinking, "I want to do a poor job today." That is just not human nature. Unfortunately, circumstances beyond teacher control frequently interfere with planning and roads paved with good intentions. More than ever, teachers need to possess an expanded repertoire of people skills, content knowledge, and instructional techniques to address the needs of at-risk students.

Special Needs

For a variety of reasons, two being the Individuals with Disabilities Education Act (IDEA) and No Child Left Behind (NCLB), more students with diagnosed disabilities (physical, psychological, and educational) are being included in general education classes than ever before. For some of these students, this may be their first experience in a general education classroom. For some teachers, it may be their first opportunity to have a student who has autism, bipolar disorder, or Down syndrome. To say this is a challenging undertaking for both parties is quite an understatement.

- How do you arrange a classroom to accommodate the student who has cerebral palsy, is in a wheelchair, and brings her service dog to school every day?
- What seat will be the best for the student who is highly distractible?
- Where do you find age-appropriate American government materials for an 18-year-old who reads at the third-grade level?
- Is there a behavior plan in place for the student who has been recently released from a treatment facility?

Students with disabilities have accommodations and modifications spelled out in detail on their Individualized Education Program (IEPs), which must be in place in the classroom. These are not mere "suggestions." They are required supports decided on by the student's IEP team and part of a legal document, the IEP. It is critical for general education teachers to attend IEP meetings to keep the dialogue flowing between them, parents, and special education case managers if these students are expected to make significant progress.

Math Anxiety

Frequently, students have such difficulty hurdling their previous math failures that they cannot see themselves having a positive experience in their current classroom. One very capable middle school student's anxiety was so high that he would lock his arms and legs around the door frame in his special education classroom when it was time to leave for math class. Another student acted out constantly in his algebra class; he said he felt better being labeled "bad" than "stupid." Within any classroom there will always be a student who sits with head down praying to be ignored or one who act outs hoping to be sent to the hall to avoid another failure.

Reading Deficits

If mathematics instruction involved only calculations, life would be less stressful for students with poor reading skills. Unfortunately, that is not the case. Textbooks have lengthy explanations and word problems; worksheets and test papers have directions that need to be deciphered and followed. Students who have reading disabilities, who read significantly below grade level, or who read very slowly are frequently stymied by the words, even though they may have the ability to do the calculations. Will they admit that to the teacher? Probably not. They will struggle with the work, copy from other students, or misinterpret what they read and complete the assignment incorrectly. This can also be true of English language learners (ELL). Although they may be capable math students when working in their own language, language barriers can develop into math barriers. All of these roads lead to frustration, and eventually some of these students will give up. To get a small taste of the impact poor reading can have on learning, try reading a textbook outside of your curricular area very-slowly-and-one-word-at-a-time. Read-one-full-page-at-that-rate-and-then-see-how-much-you-can-remember. Chances are good that by the time you reach the bottom of the page, you will not be able to recall the information at the top.

Gaps in Basic Skills

In addition to students with disabilities, learning gaps commonly occur with students who change schools frequently, who have a history of poor attendance, or who have been victims of social promotion without mastering content. As with any structure, a student's math foundation needs to be solid and intact; gaps weaken the structure.

- *Frequent School Changes:* The high school freshman who has been in the foster care system and attended nine different elementary schools will probably have significant learning gaps. Whatever the reason for "school hopping," the result is frequently the same for the student. He becomes the new face in a new place moving at a new pace. The scope and sequence of the new class may be radically different from those in his previous school. Consequently, the student may revisit a topic he already covered in October but may have just missed a topic his previous teacher was planning for January.
- *Poor Attendance:* It is very difficult for students who have missed weeks of school to have the necessary foundation on which to build future math concepts. Although reasons for frequent absences run the gamut from illness to family crisis to drug involvement, the end result is usually the same, more learning gaps.

- ***Social Promotion:*** At the elementary and middle school levels, it is not uncommon for students to be passed along to the next grade in spite of failing core classes. Those students do not possess the full range of skills needed to be successful at the next level or, in many cases, the maturity to realize their dilemma.

Language and Cultural Differences

The classrooms within our country are rapidly becoming more multicultural in their makeup, and the influx of students for whom English is not their first language has presented many challenges for educators. While some of these students arrive with a working knowledge of English as their second language, others arrive with limited fluency. This adds an additional obstacle to any subject, because now they must learn new content along with learning a new language. In addition, language barriers may keep parents from establishing a home–school communication line. The student himself, or an aunt or uncle living outside the home, may be the only English-speaking link with the family. For other students coming from home countries devastated by natural disaster or political unrest, they may have gone for periods of time where attending school was not possible. This could add even further to the difficulty of their transition.

Family Issues

In a perfect world, every student comes from a comfortable home with two supportive parents. In the real world, a student may be temporarily living with grandparents or friends while parents deal with divorce or incarceration. Finances may make it impossible for a student to purchase a calculator and other necessary materials. A single mom of four may be working multiple jobs to keep food on the table and pay for electricity, leaving no money to purchase the glasses her daughter desperately needs to be successful in school. Illness of a family member may result in frequent absences as the student babysits, helps out at home, or gets a job. There is no quick fix for family problems, but these students will need an expanded support system.

Difficulty Focusing or Maintaining Concentration

The high school student who works in a fast-food restaurant until midnight every night is going to have difficulty making good progress in a first-period algebra class. The student who has decided on his own to go off his attention-deficit disorder meds will probably have issues with geometry proofs. A highly distractible student seated at the back of the room will find more entertaining scenarios to watch than the lesson unfolding at the front of the class. A pregnant 15-year-old will spend more time worrying about how her family will react to her pregnancy than following an in-class review for tomorrow's test.

This is obviously not a definitive list of reasons that students struggle in math classes. There are as many reasons as there are struggling students. The teacher needs to focus on supporting these students with well-designed lessons, an open attitude, and a willingness to keep trying until something clicks. With all students, but especially at-risk students, the teacher needs to make opportunities to interact. Make a daily effort to have a brief conversation. Find a positive comment for the student who seems to have no friends. Toss out words of encouragement frequently. They do not cost a penny, but their value is immeasurable. You *do* have to reach them to teach them!

CHAPTER 2

10 Obstacles to Success and Their Solutions

Every fall teachers embark on a 10-month adventure with active, sluggish, gifted, confused, lonely, outgoing teenagers. Some of the students expect the trip of a lifetime; others plan to sneak out of the car at the first stop. Do not give them reasons to give up before they even begin.

Think about something you know is good for you but is not always fun, like exercise. How many obstacles can you come up with in 30 seconds that would interfere with your workout?

- It is too hot, cold, rainy, windy, early, late.
- You need to do the laundry, run errands, mow the lawn, clean the garage.
- Your exercise buddy has the flu, is out of town, left without you.

Students can quickly generate a similar list of reasons they are not succeeding in school. Many stumbling blocks for students are obvious and were discussed in chapter 1; others are much more subtle. Keep your eyes open for lack of progress and ask, "Why?" As an example, Susie, a high school senior, was having particular difficulty on algebra tests even though she had reviewed thoroughly and knew the material. She could not maintain focus for more than a few minutes at a time. The problem was that the teacher printed all tests on bright yellow paper. The contrast between the paper color and the dark font was hard for her to look at for an extended time. After her test was recopied onto white paper, she did much better. The following 10 obstacles are well within the teacher's control, are easily resolved, and will have an immediate, positive impact on many students when remedied.

Obstacle 1: Cluttered Handouts, Tests, and Quizzes

For students with visual impairments or attention-deficit disorder, cluttered handouts often appear to be a jumble of words not worth deciphering. Even in a tight economy, it is still OK to have white space on a handout.

Solution: Clearly defined sections cue students that different types of problems are coming. Design handouts and tests with white space between questions and sections. If your entire test is in Arial font, use Arial Black for titles, directions, and items you want to emphasize. Group similar problems together. Use one-inch margins or larger. See **Order of Operations** (Activity 35).

Obstacle 2: No Room for Answers

We have all been in the class where the teacher expects a full-sentence answer on a two-inch line. You try to write as small as you can to fit the information on the line or draw arrows leading to white space elsewhere on the page. Your best ideas usually do not fit in tiny spaces, and even if you can wedge them into the space, nobody besides you can read them.

Solution: Give adequate space for students to write answers. Many students, especially students with disabilities, write poorly and very large. If you hope to be able to decipher the answer, give the student enough vertical *and* horizontal space to write it, as in **Parallel Lines and Transversals** (Activity 36). As an alternative, display problems in a grid on the page to help students show their work appropriately and avoid spacing issues, as in **Fraction Interaction** (Activity 20).

Obstacle 3: Cursive

In this age of technology and texting, many students do not write in cursive and thus have difficulty reading it even if the penmanship is flawless.

Solution: Use typewritten, not handwritten materials. Do not use script fonts or cute fonts; stick with something traditional in a 12–14 font size for all handouts and tests. If you don't have access to a computer or you are writing on the board, print legibly. The same applies to comments written on students' papers. If you think it is important enough to write down, print it so they can read it.

Obstacle 4: Presentation Materials That Are Too Small

How many times have you attended an in-service where the presenter said, "I know you probably can't all read this from the back of the auditorium, but …." If you cannot see it, your interest level drops off rapidly.

Solution: Design group instructional materials to be easily read from all parts of the room. Usually a clean font like Arial 18 or 20 can be seen by everyone. See "Like Terms Graphic Organizer" in **Combining Like Terms** (Activity 21).

Obstacle 5: Poor Graph Paper

Graphing is difficult enough for students when they can see what they are doing. If your graphs are copied from copies of copies done 10 years ago, it is time to get new graph paper!

Solution: Use good graph paper with large grids, clear lines, and distinct axes. See **Linear Equations 1** (Activity 26). Make sure the information you are asking the student to graph actually fits within the graph's boundaries. It is less confusing if each square on the grid represents one unit instead of two, three, or five. See **Linear Equations 4** (Activity 29).

Obstacle 6: No Routine

A certain amount of structure is good for everyone. Structure reduces anxiety. If every day in your classroom is a brand-new adventure with no resemblance to the day before, many students will be frustrated and confused.

Solution: Early in the year, establish a daily routine for your class. Let your class become like a favorite CD where you always know what song is coming next. Once you establish the order in which things will be done, infuse variety and creativity into the instructional activities themselves.

Obstacle 7: Readability Level of Teacher-Generated Materials

Face it, you have spent years in college classes trying to impress professors with $10 words, complex sentence structure, and "college-speak." It is easy to write over the heads of students who are poor readers.

Solution: Check the readability level of your handouts. In Microsoft Word, you can set the program to give Flesch-Kincaid readability statistics after each spell check. Search the Help section to find instructions on how to do this. If the reading level is too high, use smaller words and short, simple sentences instead of compound or complex ones. The readability level of this paragraph is 8.7. Try to keep instructional materials at the fifth-grade level or below for at-risk students.

Obstacle 8: Class Notes

Students who write or process information slowly can spend entire class periods copying overhead notes and never hearing the teacher's words or participating in class discussions.

Solution: Develop note-taking organizers to help students with their class notes. An organizer helps them identify and arrange key concepts while decreasing the amount of writing they must do. For students who are poor spellers or slow writers, have some of the information already typed into the grids. That way, not only do they get to come up for air every now and then, they also see what good notes should look like. And, finally, remember that you can talk much faster than they can write. Slow down and periodically wait for stragglers. Two note-taking organizers are included in chapter 7: **Basic Geometry Terms** (Activity 1) and **Defining Angles** (Activity 5).

Obstacle 9: The "WELCOME" Mat Is Not Out

Remember your favorite aunt when you were growing up? She made you feel like the most important person in the world every time you visited her. Even though you might not have done extraordinary things with her, she was always energetic and excited about going for walks, playing cards, or just talking to you about how school was going. Be that aunt! Students really don't care if you have a master's degree in mathematics; they just want to know that you enjoy teaching and that you are glad to see them every day.

Solution: A great basketball coach routinely reminded his players to give six positive comments to each other before giving one negative comment. This applies to the classroom also. Find opportunities to interact with students in a positive way. Greet them at the classroom door. Comment on their new shoes and haircut. Ask how the football team is doing. Act excited about the lesson you are presenting. Grade papers at home and use class time to "work the room," giving support and feedback. Make eye contact when students come up to talk to you. If they look upset, ask why. Praise effort and progress. Remember to put the "WELCOME" mat out for parents too!

Obstacle 10: Individualized Education Program Accommodations and Modifications

It puts special education students in an awkward position to have to remind the teacher that they need a test reader or extended time. Given that scenario, the majority of students will forego the support to avoid embarrassment and keep a low profile.

Solution: Know your students' Individualized Education Program (IEP) accommodations and modifications. With the increasing number of special education students in general education classes, a simple chart like **Individualized Education Program Accommodations and Modifications,** on the following page, can be very helpful in tracking these necessary supports. Six blank spaces have been provided at the end of the table for you to write in accommodations and modifications that must be addressed but are not already listed.

Students' Names	Additional Time	Tests Read Aloud	Alternate Setting for Tests	Modify Test Length/Format	Monitor Long-Term Assignments	Use Calculator on All Work	Preferential Seating	Provide Copies of Class Notes	Retake Tests	Weekly Home Communication	Use Math Journals or Class Notes on Tests	Provide Study Guide Prior to Tests	Monitor Daily Planner						

FIGURE 2.1 Individualized Education Program Accommodations and Modifications

CHAPTER 3

Getting the Most Out of the
First Week of School

As your new students file in, never assume prior knowledge, specific math vocabulary, or calculator competency. You will always be surprised.

- "How do you put that dot thingy in the calculator?"
- "I thought that sign meant subtract not negative."
- "When you FOIL, which one is the outer?"
- "Where's the OFF button on this calculator?"

The first week of school is a critical time for both the student and the teacher. Students face a new array of classes and teacher expectations. Teachers have to disseminate supply lists, course outlines, textbooks, and class rules while matching names to 150 new faces. Just as important as the outflow of information *to* students, though, is the opportunity to gather information *from* students. Before relevant lessons can be planned, you need to get to know your students and their abilities. Since everyone is new to the situation, it is a perfect time to ask questions. Instead of being surprised in October that they can't divide fractions on their calculators, find out now!

Provide Opportunities for Immediate Success

Develop several first-week activities that provide opportunities for immediate success while also supplying you with information on students' personalities, math backgrounds, learning styles, confidence levels, and study habits. **Hello, My Name Is...** (Activity 16) is a short getting-to-know-you activity that can be used at any level and can be adapted to gather any information you need. Another fun first-week activity is **Info Circles** (Activity 17). Data gathered from this activity can be used later in the year to design different types of tables, charts, and graphs. It will also give students an opportunity to move around the classroom a bit and get to know each other. **Find the Sign** (Activity 15) is a check of students' knowledge of basic math symbols. It is designed to be used as a warm-up activity and should go quickly. This sheet includes items from both algebra and geometry, so some of the symbols may be ones the students have not yet had an opportunity to learn. In those cases, offer bonus points to students who do know them. Or you might choose to construct a similar survey containing only selected symbols. **Alpha Math** (Activity 14) can be done as a 15-minute competition either individually or with partners. Students earn one point for each math-related word they can add to the chart. Although it seems elementary, it can be used at any math level; the words will just increase in complexity. To reduce frustration, allow students to use their own paper for the activity if their writing is large. For lower-ability students, you can even allow textbooks or teamwork for the last few minutes of the activity. Although these activities do not directly address curriculum content, they are a quick way to ascertain which students might need additional support and monitoring throughout the year.

Do an Informal Skills Survey

Just as you would not leave town in a car with bald tires or an oil leak, you need to assess the skill level of your students before beginning instruction. Since you have students in your class from other districts and states, as well as your own feeder schools, it is impossible to outguess their levels. Develop a quick diagnostic tool like **Skills Survey** (Activity 19) that pinpoints prerequisite skills and terminology you feel your students should have already mastered. Decrease anxiety by telling the students you do not expect them to know all of the information right now and that they will retake the survey at the end of the year to see their progress. You can also use this survey to quickly assess the levels of new students who move into your class later in the year.

Check for Calculator Proficiency

Not every student who arrives in class with a scientific calculator knows how to use it. Face it, some of them bought it just for the games! Spending one class period early in the year doing a calculator refresher activity will save hours of frustration later. Make sure every student can identify the functions of the main keys and can perform basic calculations with whole numbers, decimals, and fractions. **Key In to This** (Activity 18) targets this objective.

Motivate

Develop a motivational acronym for the year. Put each letter on a separate piece of cardstock and display the acronym at the front of the room. Explain to students what an acronym is but do not reveal what the letters stand for until the end of the week. Let them ponder. After a few days, explain the acronym and discuss how it relates to their success in your class. From that moment on, anytime you need to give a pep talk, you can do it with one word.

YOGOWYPI (pronounced yō–gō–wi–pē) is an acronym developed by Bill Cordes, a speaker, consultant, and author of *The YOGOWYPI Factor*. It stands for "You only get out what you put in," a good motto for any classroom.

CHAPTER 4

Keeping Students Engaged with "Best Practices Tweaked"

Learning styles as well as dominant intelligences vary from student to student. Be aware of this and throughout the course of every week dish up something for everyone. Try something new. On television we hear stories about musicians who continually "reinvent" themselves and stay around for decades. If reinventing works for musicians, it can work for teachers, too. Rock on!

Know and Share the Objective(s) of the Day Orally and in Writing

How many times on a family trip do kids ask, "Are we there yet?" If your math objectives are written on the board and you start class by telling the students where you are going today, they will not have to ask. They will know when they arrive at their destination; it should not be a daily surprise.

Talk to Yourself and Teach Thinking: Metacognition

Math is not a spectator sport; it requires active student participation. Remember when you were first taught how to use Microsoft Word or your school's electronic grade book? If the technology trainer simply did demos and rattled off shortcut keys like Ctrl-C and Ctrl-V, you were probably left dazed and confused. Invite students inside your head to hear your thought processes. Use self-talk to model the problem-solving strategies you want them to employ when working alone. Repeat the same phrasing problem after problem to reinforce the process. Periodically leave out words or a step and signal the class to supply them for you.

Provide Adequate Wait Time

After a question, give ample wait time for student responses. There are many reasons students do not respond to a question immediately when asked. Some students are simply slow to process information and formulate a response. Perhaps others did not hear or understand the question. Fear of being wrong keeps many students, even good ones, from raising their hands. Whatever the reason, at-risk students live in hope that if they wait long enough, maybe you will just go away. Restate the question or give a hint, but be patient and wait for the answer.

Link to Prior Knowledge

Expecting students to remember a concept in isolation is like trying to organize your closet without hangers. Instead, remind them about what they already know and how those pieces link to the new concept. Give them the hanger! "Dividing fractions will be easy for you. You already know how to multiply them. To divide a pair of fractions, just remember FLIP IT-SWITCH IT. Flip the second fraction over, switch the sign to multiplication and proceed like you normally would for a multiplication problem."

Break Down Large Concepts into Small, Teachable Components

Practice breaking concepts and skills down into smaller components. There is no need to perform the Heimlich maneuver on students because they tried to take in too much information in one gulp. Offer bite-sized portions. An example of bite-size worksheets can be seen in the handouts **Factoring Quadratic Trinomials** (Activities 8–13). Not only do the pages build the process slowly, but each page utilizes the numbers and factor information produced in the initial steps. That way, students can focus on the process instead of worrying about continually generating factors for new sets of numbers.

Give Time Guidelines to Slow Workers

Think about your own life. How many times does a 5-minute task take you 30 minutes to complete? Focus! Focus! Focus! For students who have difficulty ignoring distractions, this is a major stumbling block. It helps to check in with these students periodically and give them a timeline. "You are off to a good start. I will be back around to you in five minutes, and I want to see three more problems completed."

Use Nonmathematical Props

A quick trip through your garage or kitchen can yield a multitude of math props. Bring in empty food containers and cans to calculate surface area and volume, but be prepared for some teasing about what your family eats! Play "Doodads," a quick game on the overhead projector to introduce like terms. Turn on the projector and place items like pennies, paperclips, nuts, bolts, and washers on the screen. Use a blank transparency to keep the glass from getting scratched. Then ask for volunteers to come up and group the items according to their properties. Students must give a rationale for the groupings they use: round versus not round, office items versus kitchen items, or metal versus plastic. A similar paper-and-pencil task is **Combining Like Terms** (Activity 21), where students are given a list of items commonly found at garage sales and have to decide on a strategy for grouping like items. A different activity, **Real Number System: No Leftovers** (Activity 44), uses a set of nesting food-storage containers to introduce the real numbers.

Burst into Song

Besides announcing that everyone gets a free pizza or that tomorrow's test has been cancelled, bursting into song is the next best attention-getter in a classroom. And the good news is that you don't even have to be a good singer! Sometimes just putting a couple of lines of instructions to music gets everyone's attention; it is like math opera! "Tomorrow, tomorrow, your test is tomorrow.

It's only a day away!" or "Positive, negative, zero, undefined. Oh what fun it is to graph a perfectly straight line. Hey!" ("Jingle Bells"). If you burst into song, you *will* sing alone at first. Don't let that deter you, and don't be shy. If you look like you are having fun, eventually students will join in. A quick Internet search will uncover an abundance of math songs. The quadratic formula, for example, can be sung to the tune of several familiar children's songs. You can even write your own songs. Dr. Joyce Faye Saxon and Dr. Thomas Klein, at Marshall University, wrote this excellent review of mean, median, and mode, sung to the tune of "Three Blind Mice."

The Mean, Median, and Mode Song

Mean, median, mode.
Mean, median, mode.
Central tendency.
Central tendency.
MEAN is the average of what you've got.
MEDIAN is stuck in the middle spot.
MODE's the most frequent one of the lot.
Mean, median, mode.
Mean, median, mode.

Another teacher-generated song, **Number Tag: A Real Numbers Song** (Activity 32), sung to the tune of "Jingle Bells," can be used to introduce the real numbers. Just remember, if you plan to put a concept to music, use a simple tune that everyone knows and that is easy to sing, and don't make the song more difficult than the original concept. One final warning: The major downside to teaching concepts with a song is the constant humming during exams!

Tell a Story

While your students may not remember the homework instructions you just gave, it is practically guaranteed that they will remember every fact that comes out of your mouth about your family, your vacation, and your dogs. That being said, use stories about yourself, your family, or a character you made up to illustrate a concept. Incorporate humor or a play on words. The worse the story is and the louder the groans afterward, the better the chance that the students will remember the information.

> "My brother, Perry, loved to jog on the sidewalk around the town square in the small town where he lived. Around and around he went every day, until one beautiful spring day he met 'her.' The girl of his dreams was jogging around the same square. They fell madly in love and married one year later in the park. When they grew old, they told all of their friends the story about how Perry-met-her (perimeter)."

Go ahead and groan, but you will remember the story!

Use a Picture Worth 1,000 Words

Whenever possible use a visual to introduce a new concept. Your oral explanation combined with written text and extra pictures will reach more students than any one of those delivery methods alone. Figure 4.1 illustrates a quick way to visually represent three different types of graphed equations: linear, quadratic, and absolute value.

FIGURE 4.1 Visual Cues for Graphing

Bring In Real-World Applications

Bring in real-world applications to address the perennial question, "When are we ever going to use this stuff?" To practice protractor skills, find magazine pictures that have elements in them that form strong angles. Outline the angles with a permanent marker and then laminate the pictures. You can use these for classroom practice for years, and they are much more entertaining than angles drawn on a worksheet. If you do not enjoy digging through magazines yourself, offer one bonus point for each good picture students bring in. Remember to name the maximum number they can bring, or you will have hundreds of pages!

Your **digital camera** can also be a great lesson-planning tool. A short field trip around town can yield dozens of photos of geometric figures or of positive and negative slopes. After you have taken the photos, add them to your favorite presentation software, and you have a quick review or an introduction to a new concept in an unexpected format. You could also use the photos for an interactive bulletin board, **What's Your Angle?** (Activity 48), which reinforces angle measurement, using photos like the two shown on the next page.

Act It Out

Elementary teachers across the country are using readers theater skits in their classrooms to improve reading fluency and comprehension while also addressing content. This format could be very beneficial to special education students or English language learner students who need additional math *and* reading support outside of the classroom. **Varsity Sue, a Readers Theater Play** (Activity 45) includes a short play and follow-up activity that reinforce circle terminology and how it can be used at home. The readability of the skit is 2.9.

Offer Examples and Nonexamples

If it looks like a duck and sounds like a duck, it probably *is* a duck. Let students define a new concept based both on examples and nonexamples. Remember the part-time jobs you had in high school and college? At that point in your life, while you might not have known what career you *did* want, based on summer job experiences you could quickly eliminate ones you *did not* want. Those were your career nonexamples. Look at **Characteristics of Polygons** (Activity 2). For some students, seeing what a polygon is *not* helps them clarify what it *is*. When you feel the students have developed a good understanding of polygons, have them generate their own examples and nonexamples.

Take a Different Approach

Moment of truth...when you tie your shoes, do you make bunny ears? Surely someone tried to teach you to do it that way, but maybe it just did not work for you. If a student does not understand your explanation the first time, there is always a chance she was not listening. If you reexplain it the

FIGURE 4.2 Road Work

FIGURE 4.3 Concrete Slide

same way with no increase in understanding, try something different. Sometimes, you might even preface your lesson with the comment that you will show two different methods and students can use whichever one they prefer. Tom Colley, a math teacher at Shawnee Mission Northwest High School in Kansas, developed an easy way for students to find the greatest common factor. The same process also quickly yields the least common multiple. See **Greatest Common Factor, Two Methods** (Activity 22). Two other activities that demonstrate alternate approaches are **Prime Factorization, Check-Double-Check** (Activity 40) and **Multiplying Binomials, Check-Double-Check** (Activity 34). These allow students to work with a partner, completing the same problems by two different methods, and then double-checking each other afterward.

Use Mnemonics

Every high school math student at some point has been taught "Please Excuse My Dear Aunt Sally" to learn the order of operations. **Dog-Gone Awesome Math (DGAM)** (Activity 6) is a mnemonic that students can use to solve multistep equations. DGAM stands for **D**istribute, **G**ather like terms, **A**ddress it, **M**ake it one. Another interesting memory aid, HOY-VUX, which is explained in **Linear Equations 5** (Activity 30), can be used to distinguish equations of horizontal and vertical lines. HOY is for **H**orizontal lines, **0** slope, **Y** = equations. VUX stands for **V**ertical lines, **U**ndefined slope, **X** = equations. The trick to using mnemonics or any other type of memory aid is to repeat them frequently and to not make the memory aid more difficult to remember than the original concept!

Allow Students to Use Tools

In the perfect math world of your dreams, all students will remember the formula for the surface area of a cylinder. They won't. Adults don't remember it either; they search for it on the Internet. The question then becomes, would you prefer the student be able to spout formulas or to use a reference to find the appropriate formula needed for problem solving? At the beginning of the school year, ask students to designate a section of their notebooks as a "toolbox" where they can keep helpful sheets you give them throughout the year. This will be particularly beneficial for students who have difficulty memorizing terms, facts, and formulas but are otherwise quite capable of doing the assigned math work. Tool sheets that accompany the activities in this book are noted with a wrench symbol after the title, so students can differentiate them from regular worksheets.

Visually Organize Handouts

Have you ever packed in a hurry and forgot to label all of your moving boxes? That probably made finding your silverware and underwear pretty difficult. That scenario is the way many at-risk students view teacher handouts. Visually organizing a handout's formatting (bold, italicized, underlined text) and using boxes, charts, and arrows helps students quickly key in to what information goes together and to prioritize its importance. See **Linear Equations 4** (Activity 29) and **Linear Equations 6** (Activity 31).

Make the Most of Your Bulletin Board Space

The art department does not have a monopoly on color and design elements, and teenagers still appreciate interesting, instructional bulletin boards. When students arrive on the first day of school, make them feel that they are important and that you planned for their arrival. Math classrooms should not look sterile and boring, showcasing only class rules and make-up work folders. Spend some time each quarter creating instructional, interactive, and motivational boards.

- Draw a giant refrigerator door where you can post student papers during the year. They may be teenagers, but they still love a parade in their honor.
- Post interactive bulletin boards where students can find review activities to work on if they finish their work early. See **RAP (Review-and-Practice) Cards** (Activity 43) and **What's Your Angle?** (Activity 48)
- Each quarter, design a different interactive board to reinforce your current material. Dr. R. S. Schaeffer, at Kutztown University of Pennsylvania, challenges his math education students to create interactive bulletin boards for their students. Each board has to meet five criteria. It must be educational, fun, interactive, accompanied by a worksheet, and for credit. His Web site, faculty.kutztown.edu/schaeffe/BulletinBoards/bbs.html, offers examples of his students' work, where you can examine their bulletin boards, directions, and accompanying worksheets.

Preteach Vocabulary

For many students, it is beneficial to preview all new vocabulary at the beginning of the lesson. This is especially true for students who are working significantly below grade level. **Parallel Lines and Transversals** (Activity 36) is an example of a geometry lesson modified for special education students. It pinpoints a limited number of concepts to introduce within the lesson and appeals to a variety of intelligences by introducing vocabulary with a limerick, definitions, sketches, and manipulatives. Included with this lesson is "Limericks and Lingo," which has four additional limericks that can be used to introduce other math content.

Provide Timely Feedback on Homework and Tests

Everyone agrees that teachers are busy people. As difficult as it might be to return homework and tests within a day or two, the benefits are staggering. For many at-risk students, long-term retention of material is very difficult. If it takes a week or more for the teacher to return their tests, they have probably forgotten the material by that point, so going over the tests in class is frustrating to them.

CHAPTER 5

Distributed Practice, Reviews, and Tests

Students with disabilities are generally not "big-picture" learners. In fact, their focus on the small details frequently obscures the big picture. Although they may master individual concepts on a day-to-day basis, they often do not retain or transfer skills easily from one day to the next. Thus the concepts remain scattered puzzle pieces instead of forming an assembled picture. Distributed practice and review after a lesson or a chapter are just as critical to these students' understanding of the material as the initial instruction. Without rebuilding the big picture, they might remember only the armadillo on the roadside instead of the Alamo! This opportunity to put the pile of jigsaw pieces back together into a completed puzzle can be done many ways, as illustrated by the activities discussed in this chapter.

Distributed-Practice Tips

- Start class every day with a warm-up activity that includes problems from the previous day as well as problems from a concept taught in the previous month. By continually revisiting past content, it remains fresh in the students' minds.
- Anytime you are introducing a new concept, link it to a previous concept with several practice problems. This gives a solid foundation to the new material.
- Break large topics down into small component parts and practice only one part at a time until students achieve mastery.
- Do periodic practice of basic skills.
- Establish "review days" anytime the school schedule has to be modified for assemblies, teacher conferences, and in-services, or any day when you must be gone and have a substitute. Instead of trying to introduce new content during a shortened class period, choose important previous topics to revisit.
- Make multiple versions of "critical skill" practice sheets covering topics like operations with fractions, solving equations, or graphing lines. Keep them short; 10 problems is perfect. Have students complete a different one every week until they show proficiency.

Review Tips

- Remind students to clear their desks of unnecessary and distracting materials before you start reviewing. Their focus should be totally on you and the material, not the card they just received from a friend or cosmetics from their purse.
- Do not expect students to do all of their reviewing at home. It probably will not happen, and if it does, they will not key into the same "important concepts" you would have pointed out.
- Encourage students to make flash cards for vocabulary words and formulas and practice them for 5 to 10 minutes each day.
- When going over key points, use focus words to get students' attention: "This will be on the test for sure." "Here are three things you are really going to want to write down."
- Provide a study guide with some of the information already filled in, and ask students to complete the guide as you review in class.
- If you are using a review worksheet or study guide, put the page number where the information or a similar problem can be found. This will reduce the frustration for students who are slow readers and have difficulty skimming the chapters for answers.
- As an alternative to using page numbers, put the study guide questions in chapter order. That way, when students find the answer to Question 6, they know the answer to Question 7 will follow.
- Sometimes, the hardest part of reviewing a multistep process is just getting started. **What's Your First Step?** (Activity 49) addresses that issue. Students are asked to simply identify the first step needed to solve a series of equations, not to actually solve them.
- By having students use materials you have created to do a review packet, at least you know the information they are reviewing is correct. **Parallel Lines, Transversals, and the Angles They Form** (Activity 37) is a teacher-generated summary that students can use when doing a comprehensive review activity.
- Remember to address higher-level thinking skills in your reviews. **What's the Difference?** (Activities 46 and 47) pairs up concepts that have some element in common and then asks students to explain how they are different. There are two levels of this activity, one for pre-algebra and one for algebra.
- Rapid-fire reviews will keep students on their toes. **Whatzit?** (Activity 50) has geometric sketches students must identify. The teacher calls out a letter, and the student identifies the figure. Done as team play in an elimination format, this can be a fun review.
- The **Linear Equations** packet (Activities 26–31) breaks down a very large concept into small review sections that will not overwhelm the students. For students with disabilities or who frustrate easily, give them one page at a time. When they show you that the first page is finished, give them the next one.
- Reviews do not have to be painful! Games are a fun way to keep students' attention while reviewing. The next chapter outlines several games included in chapter 7 that can also be used for review.

Test Tips

One general rule about testing that applies to all students, but particularly at-risk students, is to evaluate what they know, not their vision, their reading ability, or their frustration level.

- Check the readability level of your test in Microsoft Word. If it is above 5.0, use shorter sentences and smaller words.

- Run tests on white paper; some students have difficulty reading text on colored sheets.
- Put simple questions first to allow students to gain confidence.
- Give the test one page at a time for students who become easily overwhelmed.
- Allow breaks for those with vision, health, or attention problems.
- Provide additional time for slow readers. Allow them to start the test early or come in after school to finish it.
- Mark the "need-to-know" questions with an asterisk, a circle, or highlighting, and have students with disabilities start with those. If they do not finish the entire test, you can grade them on completion of the critical concepts.
- Some students work very slowly in spite of knowing the material. For those students, decrease the number of problems they have to do.
- If a student fails to start within a minute or two, check in with him and find out why. Sometimes students are hesitant to begin because the directions are confusing to them. Quietly and privately ask the student to repeat the directions to you before he begins and clear up any confusion at that time.
- Some students "drift off" periodically during tests. It may be an escape mechanism to help them decrease frustration, or they may not have the attention span to stay on task for a full hour. Develop a nonverbal cue, like touching the corner of their desk, to get them back on task without distracting those seated nearby.
- Be observant: Watch for signs of frustration. If you notice a pattern of this with a student, talk to him privately and come up with a plan to reduce the anxiety of testing. Allow him to leave the room for a short restroom break midway through the test, or give him only one page of the test at a time.
- *Matching Questions:* Limit matching sections to groups of 5 to 10 questions. Since we read from left to right, it is also helpful for poor readers if the wordy stem of the question is located in the left-hand column and the key word it matches is in the right-hand column. If it is reversed, by the time they have finished scanning all of the lengthy stems, they have forgotten the original word they were trying to match.
- *Multiple-Choice Questions:* Use capital letters for multiple-choice options instead of lowercase ones. This will help the students who sometimes confuse lowercase b and d. Allow students to circle answers on multiple-choice sections instead of copying them into blanks. List multiple-choice options vertically instead of side-by-side. Avoid tricky wording: double negatives, none of the above, or only B and C. If you are use words like sometimes, always, or never, underline them. It is easy for poor readers to miss one word in a statement, and those particular words can totally change the answer.
- Finally, return test papers as soon as possible and go over them in class. It is difficult to learn from your mistakes when you don't see them for two weeks. By then you have moved on to new material, and the old material has been shuffled to the back of your mind. You might also consider giving students an opportunity to correct-up tests or to retake a parallel version of the test if they did poorly.

CHAPTER 6

Sometimes It Can Be Fun and Games

Instructional games, when used correctly, can be an important component of the classroom curriculum. Well-constructed games have a wide range of educational, social, and motivational benefits:

- They nudge quiet students into a more interactive learning mode. During a typical lesson, a student can sometimes get away with being "invisible." This is more difficult when students are playing a game, especially if there are small groups involved. Use games that encourage the simultaneous involvement of as many students as possible. Down time is not <u>pro</u>ductive and in some cases can be <u>dis</u>ruptive.

- They reduce stress and anxiety by periodically breaking up the daily classroom routine. While a routine is important, if students know ahead of time that a game is coming later in the week, it can put a positive spin on the work leading up to it. A game also means that there will be no new concepts being taught and no assignment required at the end, which can be a nice reward for their hard work.

- They motivate students to practice concepts they have recently learned. While a typical high school student will probably not practice calculating the slope of linear equations for 30 minutes at home, he _will_ play a game based on that material in the classroom.

- They allow for different student groupings. Mix things up to reinforce social skills and encourage cooperation between students of different ability levels. Let the students decide on their own groups sometimes and other times you pick the teams or even draw names out of a hat.

- They allow for more movement and interaction than on a typical lesson-centered day. Remember, not all noise is bad noise!

- They ignite excitement by providing a challenge. Everybody likes to win! Most students are motivated to play games just by their own competitive nature, but others need a prize. Develop a prize menu from which students can choose: earning bonus points for a quiz or test, choosing a new seat in the classroom, or dropping one assignment at the end of the quarter. Be creative.

- They bring all the pieces of a chapter or unit together into a cohesive package. It is like the final 10 pages of a mystery novel where all of the loose ends are tied up. After spending two weeks learning "everything there is to know" about graphing linear equations, students need the time and a format in which to reassemble the pieces.

This book contains a variety of classroom game formats that can be used at any level with any topic. Each game has a full explanation of the rules as well as game cards or questions for pre-algebra, algebra, or geometry topics. Each game format has been designed to involve many students simultaneously with as little downtime as possible. A brief description of each game follows.

Cubes

This is a whole-class game that can have as many as six winners each time it is played. Choose one of three game boards with empty squares. Students use a sheet prepared by the teacher to fill in each square of their game board with possible answers to math questions. As the teacher reads the questions, if the student has the correct answer, he circles it. The goal is to be the first person to get a line of answers correct. The game topics are listed in the following.

- **Cubes** (Activity 3): This pre-algebra game includes questions focusing on patterns, order of operations, expressions and equations, factors and multiples, and divisibility rules.
- **Cubes** (Activity 4): This algebra game focuses on linear equations and includes questions about slope, intercepts, and parallel and perpendicular lines.

Gridlock

This is a partner puzzle game where students are asked to reassemble puzzle pieces into a grid by pairing up mathematical items. The winner is the first team to assemble the puzzle correctly. The game topics are identified in the activities' titles.

- **Gridlock: Fractions, Decimals, and Percentages** (Activity 23): Pre-algebra
- **Gridlock: Like Terms** (Activity 24): Algebra
- **Gridlock: Geometry Terms** (Activity 25): Geometry

Pass It On

This is a "row race" game where students pass a game sheet backwards through their row, with each person choosing a problem to complete. The questions on the game sheet should be ones that can be answered in less than a minute to keep the game moving along quickly. The winner is the row that gets the most problems correct. The game topics are listed here.

- **Pass It On: Plotting Ordered Pairs** (Activity 38): Pre-algebra
- **Pass It On: Geometric Shapes** (Activity 39): Geometry

Quads

In this game, students are asked to work together in teams of four to answer content-related questions. All team members must agree on answers before they can be submitted. Questions can be drawn from almost any homework assignment or supplementary worksheet you have been using. The winner is the quad that gets the most problems correct.

- **Quads** (Activity 42): Algebra (linear equations)

CHAPTER 7

Activities, Teacher Pages, and Solutions

All of the activities discussed in chapters 1–6 are included as blackline masters in this chapter. The "Table of Activities" chart at the beginning of the book lists each activity's title, number, and content. The levels highlighted to the right of each title indicate whether the activity is appropriate for **P**re-Algebra, **A**lgebra, or **G**eometry. A teacher page accompanies each activity. The teacher pages include special directions, teacher tips, and solutions.

LESSON

Basic Geometry Terms: Teacher Page

Content: Note sheet for basic geometry terms

Standard(s):

	Activity 1	
P	**A**	**G**

About This Activity . . .	**Solutions**

This note-taking format is beneficial for students with significant language or spelling deficits and those who write or process information slowly. It allows them to follow along with the introduction of new material with minimal writing. Students with disabilities need frequent repetition and practice of materials to attain mastery. Concepts they are confident with one day often seem like brand-new material to them the next day. Follow up note taking by encouraging those students to make a set of flash cards for geometry terms, figures, and formulas and to review the cards for 10 minutes each day. This will significantly improve their long-term retention of the material. Be sure to use lined 3×5 cards. They are easy to manipulate, work well for students with large writing, and are not as easy to misplace as smaller flash cards.

| Collinear Points |
| • • • • |
| (front) |

| Points located on the same line |
| (back) |

Flash cards are obviously not restricted to special education students or to geometry; they can be used successfully by any student at any level.

Solutions

1. •
2. ←——→
3. • • • •
4. •——•
5. •——→
6. •——•
7. (arrow diagram)
8. (arrow diagram)
9. (dashed arrow diagram)
10. (parallelogram labeled P)
11. (crossed arrows diagram)

From *Making Math Accessible for the At-Risk Student: Grades 7–12* by Linda Ptacek. Santa Barbara, CA: Libraries Unlimited. Copyright © 2011.

LESSON

Basic Geometry Terms: Student Note Sheet

Name: _____ Date: _____ Hr: _____

	Term	**Sketch**	**Definition**
1.	Point		An exact location in space
2.	Line		A collection of points in a straight path that goes forever in opposite directions
3.	Collinear points		Points that are located on the same line
4.	Line segment		A part of a line that contains two endpoints and all the points between them
5.	Ray		A part of a line that has one endpoint and goes forever in only one direction
6.	Endpoint		A point at the beginning or end of a line segment
7.	Angle		The figure formed by two rays that share a common endpoint
8.	Vertex of an angle		The common endpoint of two rays that form an angle
9.	Sides of an angle		The rays that form an angle
10.	Plane		A flat surface that extends forever in all directions
11.	Intersect		To cross or meet each other at one point

LESSON

Characteristics of Polygons: Teacher Page

Content: Introduction of attributes of polygons through examples and nonexamples

Standard(s):

About This Activity . . .	**Solutions**
The purpose of this activity is to discover the critical attributes of a polygon by looking at both examples and nonexamples. Ask the students to pair up, moving their desks next to each other, and give each person a copy of the student handout. Allow several minutes for the partners to examine and discuss the sketches, and then on the blank side of one of their handouts ask them to list what they believe to be the important characteristics of polygons. When all pairs have finished, ask each pair to share one of the ideas they had written down. Then as a group, pinpoint the three characteristics they should all write on lines 1–3 on the front of the handout:	**1.** at left below **2.** at left below **3.** at left below **4.** polygon **5.** not a polygon **6.** not a polygon **7.** polygon **8.** not a polygon **9.** not a polygon **10.** answers will vary **11.** answers will vary
1. Polygons must be closed figures.	
2. Polygons must be made up of straight line segments.	
3. The line segments making a polygon can only meet at their endpoints; they cannot cross.	
Ask students to then complete the worksheet with their partners. When they have finished, go through Questions 4–9, asking students to explain why the figures are or are not polygons. Then ask for volunteers to draw answers to Questions 10 and 11 on the board.	

LESSON

Characteristics of Polygons: Student Handout

Activity 2

| P | A | G |

Name: _____ Date: _____ Hr: _____

These Are Polygons		These Are NOT Polygons	

Based on the sketches above, what characteristics do all polygons share?

1. _____

2. _____

3. _____

Which figures below are polygons? _____

4.   **5.**   **6.**   **7.**   **8.**   **9.**

10. Draw two polygons below.   **11.** Draw two figures below that are <u>not</u> polygons.

Cubes: Teacher Page

Content: Various pre-algebra and algebra topics in two different games

Standard(s):

Quick view: This class game can have several winners each time it is played. Three game board options are offered. Students use the "solutions" sheet provided by the teacher to fill in each square of their game board with possible answers to math questions. As questions are read by the teacher, students circle the correct answers on their game boards. The goal is to be the first person to get a row of answers circled.

The set-up: Run a copy of the questions for yourself and a game board and solutions sheet for each student. Allow five minutes before the game begins for students to copy answers from the "solutions" sheet onto their grids. There will be more answers than they have spaces for on the grid. Remind them to be careful not to use any answer more than once.

The play: Randomly select questions from the question sheet to read. Ask students to circle the answer on the game board if they have it. Play continues until a student has circled and "taken" a line of boxes on his sheet. Stop briefly to verify that the answers he has circled are correct and then continue asking questions. Once a row is taken, that line is then off-limits as a winning line. Continue until other students have taken the remaining available lines. The game ends when all cubes are taken by a player. A player may win for only <u>one line</u> of cubes but may win again for being the first person to take <u>all</u> cubes. That way all students are motivated to continue playing for the duration of the game.

Special note: If you plan to design additional sets of questions for this game, always have twice as many questions as you have cubes.

Cubes: Pre-Algebra Game Board

Activity 3		
P	**A**	**G**

You can win by getting a line of answers or the shaded triangle of answers.

REVIEW GAME

Cubes: Pre-Algebra Game Board

REVIEW GAME

Cubes: Pre-Algebra Solutions

		Activity 3	
P	**A**	**G**	

Student Directions: You have five minutes to choose from these answers to fill in your game board. Cross them out after you use them, so you do not accidentally use them twice.

$\frac{4}{3}$	$\frac{5}{4}$	10	1, 2, 3, 6	equation
3^2	5	−8	10 and 15	expression
16	15	13	7	Commutative
9	4	factor	true	improper
$2\frac{4}{5}$	3	14	1	17
44	85	25	$\frac{3}{4}$	$\frac{23}{7}$
12	☺	false	$\frac{5}{11}$	.4
yes	5 and 7	$\frac{5}{12}$	prime	$\frac{1}{3}$
mean	30	solve	.5	11
mode	21	no	8	2

Cubes: Pre-Algebra Game Questions and Solutions

1. What is next in this sequence? 100, 95, 90, ___ **85**

2. Simplify $6 \times 2 + 9$. **21**

3. Is this an expression or an equation: $-12x$? . . . . **expression**

4. Evaluate 4^2. . . . . . **16**

5. List all of the factors of 6. . . . . . . **1, 2, 3, 6**

6. Is 8 a solution to $4x - 12 = 20$? . . . . **yes**

7. What comes next? ☺ ☹ ☺ ☹ ___ . . . . . . ☺

8. Calculate $4 \times 3 + 10 \div 5$. **14**

9. Is the following an expression or an equation? $4x - 4 = 12$. . . . . . . **equation**

10. Evaluate ab if $a = 6$ and $b = 5$. **30**

11. Is 13 prime or composite? . . . . **prime**

12. Name the property shown: $7 + 10 = 10 + 7$. . . . . . . **Commutative**

13. Simplify $2 + (10 + 20) \div 5$. **8**

14. What is 50% of 30? **15**

15. Divide $\frac{2}{3}$ by $\frac{1}{2}$ . . . . $\frac{4}{3}$

16. Is 3 a factor of 103? . . . . **no**

17. True or false: 136 is divisible by 9. . . . . . . **false**

18. What is the next term in this sequence? . . . . . . .48, 24, 12, 6 . . . . **3**

19. What is the first step: $7 + 3^2 - 12 \div 4$. . . . . . **3^2**

20. Do you solve or evaluate an equation? . . . . **solve**

21. Evaluate $(2 + 3)^2$. **25**

22. Name two multiples of 5. . . . . . . **10 and 15**

23. To fill in the blank to make 123__ divisible by 4, would you use 2 or 5?. **2**

24. What comes next in this sequence? . . . . . . .1, 1, 2, 3, 5, 8 . . . **13**

25. What is the reciprocal of $\frac{4}{5}$? . . . . $\frac{5}{4}$

26. Reduce $\frac{20}{48}$ to lowest terms. . . . . . . $\frac{5}{12}$

27. What is the reciprocal of $2\frac{1}{5}$? . . . . $\frac{5}{11}$

From Making Math Accessible for the At-Risk Student: Grades 7–12 by Linda Ptacek. Santa Barbara, CA: Libraries Unlimited. Copyright © 2011.

28. Name two prime factors of 35. . . . . . . **5 and 7**

29. To fill in the blank to make 247___ divisible by 9, would you use 2 or 5?. . . . **5**

30. What is the decimal equivalent of $\frac{1}{2}$? . . . . **.5**

31. What is the fraction equivalent of .75? . . . . $\frac{3}{4}$

32. What is $\frac{4}{12}$ reduced to lowest terms? . . . . $\frac{1}{3}$

33. What is $\frac{14}{5}$ as a mixed number? . . . . $2\frac{4}{5}$

34. What is the mean of 4, 9, and 8? **7**

35. What is the median of 5, 9, 10, 33, and 45? **10**

36. Round 43.6 to the nearest whole number. **44**

37. Round .3571 to the nearest tenth. . . . . . . **.4**

38. What is the missing factor of 8: 2, 4, 8? **1**

39. Which of these is an integer: $\frac{1}{2}$ or –8? . . . . **–8**

40. What is the range of the digits on a standard clock? **11**

41. What is the mode for this data set: 9, 11, 12, 10, 9. . . . . . . **9**

42. Name the integer between 16.2 and 17.5. . . . . . . **17**

43. True or false: 1, 2, 4, 8, and 16 are all factors of 16. . . . . **true**

44. Is 932 divisible by 3 or by 4? **4**

45. Change $3\frac{2}{7}$ to an improper fraction? . . . . $\frac{23}{7}$

46. Is $\frac{3}{2}$ a proper or improper fraction? . . . . **improper**

47. What integer can also be written as $\frac{24}{2}$? **12**

48. What do you call the number that occurs most often in a set of data? . . . . **mode**

49. Finding the "average" is the same as calculating the _____. . . . . . . **mean**

50. What do you call a number that will divide evenly into another number? . . . .
factor

From *Making Math Accessible for the At-Risk Student: Grades 7–12* by Linda Ptacek. Santa Barbara, CA: Libraries Unlimited. Copyright © 2011.

Cubes: Algebra Game Board

Winning Slopes

You must have a line of correct answers and call out the underlined slope word to win!

Positive: Correct answers on the diagonal from bottom left to top right
Negative: Correct answers on the diagonal from top left to bottom right
Zero: Correct answers on any horizontal line
Undefined: Correct answers on any vertical line

REVIEW GAME

Cubes: Algebra Game Solutions

Activity 4		
P	A	G

Directions: You have five minutes to choose from these answers to fill in your game board. Cross them out after you use them, so you do not accidentally use them again.

HOY-VUX	$\frac{1}{2}$	same	$\perp$	$\dfrac{y_2 - y_1}{x_2 - x_1}$
(0, 10) (–6, 0)	2	pair	no	yes
side-to-side	y	There is not one.	slope	y = mx + b
reciprocals	–7	origin	A ∥ B	zero
quadrants	3	vertical	false	m
horizontal	–9	–2	$\frac{1}{7}$	10
standard	true	(23, 0)	5	x
undefined	(0, –11)	range	domain	(0, –9) (6, 0)
y-intercept	$-\frac{3}{5}$	–4	linear	x = –2
up and down	b	$\frac{1}{9}$	y = –2	run

From *Making Math Accessible for the At-Risk Student: Grades 7–12* by Linda Ptacek. Santa Barbara, CA: Libraries Unlimited. Copyright © 2011.

Cubes: Algebra Game Questions and Solutions

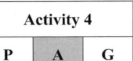

1. The steepness of a line is called its _____. . . . . . . **slope**

2. Parallel lines have the ____ slope. . . . . . **same**

3. What do you call the point where a line crosses the y-axis? . . . . **y-intercept**

4. What kind of line has a zero slope? . . . . **horizontal**

5. What mnemonic device helps you remember horizontal and vertical lines? . . . . **HOY-VUX**

6. Slope is sometimes expressed as rise over ____. . . . . . . **run**

7. What is the slope of a line parallel to $y = -7x - 2$? . . . . **–7**

8. What is the slope of a line perpendicular to $y = -7x - 2$? . . . . $\frac{1}{7}$

9. What kind of line has an undefined slope? . . . . **vertical**

10. An equation that makes a straight line when graphed is called _____ . . . . **linear**

11. Find the slope of a line through (2, 9) and (7, 6). . . . . . . $-\frac{3}{5}$

12. What is the y-intercept of the equation $y = 16x - 2$? . . . . **–2**

13. A slope of $\frac{1}{3}$ has a run of ___. **3**

14. Perpendicular lines have slopes that are opposite ___. . . . . . . **reciprocals**

15. What is the y-intercept of the line $y = -4x + 5$? **5**

16. What is the slope of the line $y = \frac{1}{2}x - 3$? . . . . $\frac{1}{2}$

17. What is the slope of the line $y = 8$? . . . . . . **zero**

18. What is the slope of the line $x = -7$? . . . . **undefined**

19. If two lines have slopes of –2 and $\frac{1}{2}$ will they intersect? . . . . **yes**

20. True or false: There are only two kinds of slope: positive or negative. . . . . **false**

21. What is the slope of a line perpendicular to $y = \frac{1}{4}x + 8$? . . . . **–4**

22. Find the x and y intercepts of the equation $6x - 4y = 36$. . . . . **(0, –9) (6, 0)**

23. In the equation $y = mx + b$ what letter stands for the slope? . . . . **m**

24. In the equation y = mx + b what letter stands for the y-intercept? . . . . **b**

25. What mathematical shortcut says lines A and B are parallel? . . . . **A ∥ B**

26. What is the mathematical symbol for perpendicular? . . . . **⊥**

27. What is the y-intercept of the line x = 7? . . . . **There is not one.**

28. What is the slope-intercept form? . . . . **y = mx + b**

29. Find the y-intercept of this equation by solving for y.   x + 2y = 20. . . . . **10**

30. True or false: An example of a gradual slope is $\frac{1}{10}$ . . . . **true**

31. An equation like 4x + 2y = 10 is in _____ form. . . . . **standard**

32. The point (0,0) on the coordinate grid is called the _____ . . . . **origin**

33. The coordinate axis is divided into four sections called _____ . . . . **quadrants**

34. Which axis runs up and down? . . . . **y**

35. Which axis runs left to right? . . . . **x**

36. In a table of values, the x-values are called the _____ . . . . **domain**

37. In a table of values, the y-values are called the _____ . . . . **range**

38. What is the equation of a horizontal line at –2? . . . . **y = –2**

39. What is the equation of a vertical line at –2? . . . . **x = –2**

40. Find the slope of a line through (7, 4) and (6, 2). **2**

41. (3, –7) is called an "ordered _____." . . . . **pair**

42. Is x = –5 a horizontal line? Yes or no. . . . . . . **no**

43. Find the x- and y-intercepts of the equation –5x + 3y = 30. . . . . **(0, 10) (–6, 0)**

44. What is the slope of a line parallel to y = –9x + 3? . . . . **–9**

45. What is the slope of a line perpendicular to y = –9x + 3? . . . . $\frac{1}{9}$

46. What point is the y-intercept for the equation y = –11? . . . . **(0, –11)**

47. What point is the x-intercept for the equation x = 23? . . . . **(23, 0)**

48. Does *horizontal* mean "up and down" or "side to side"? . . . . **side to side**

49. Does *vertical* mean "up and down" or "side to side"? . . . . **up and down**

50. What is the formula to calculate slope given two points? . . . . . . $\dfrac{\mathbf{y_2 - y_1}}{\mathbf{x_2 - x_1}}$

Defining Angles: Teacher Page

Activity 5		
P	**A**	**G**

Content: Acute, right, obtuse, straight, reflex, complementary, supplementary, adjacent, vertical, linear pair

Standard(s):

About This Activity . . .

This is a three-part review of angle types. Begin by using the note-taking sheet to review nine types of angles. The terms and the definitions are already given, so students only need to sketch the figures. After the angles have been sketched and discussed, pass out the "Check for Understanding" sheet. Use this page to quickly practice identifying the angle types. Go through the page twice as a class, randomly calling out numbers to be identified and asking for a group response. After the group check, have students use their note sheets and a blank piece of paper to individually identify the angles on the "Check for Understanding" handout. When you are confident that the students know the angle types, pass out the student worksheet. Have them work on this individually. Remind students that naming angles is like naming people. You can easily get angles confused if you do not give their first, middle, and last names (three points, with the vertex as the middle name). The answers for the "Check for Understanding" page are listed at right. Answers for the student worksheet are not given, as they will vary widely.

Solutions to "Check for Understanding"

1. complementary
2. right
3. vertical
4. acute
5. straight
6. adjacent
7. obtuse
8. right
9. obtuse
10. vertical
11. supplementary
12. reflex
13. reflex
14. acute
15. complementary
16. adjacent
17. supplementary
18. straight

LESSON

Defining Angles: Student Note Sheet

Name: _____ Date: _____ Hr: _____

	Term	Sketch	Definition
1.	Acute angle		An angle measuring less than 90°
2.	Right angle		An angle measuring exactly 90°
3.	Obtuse angle		An angle measuring more than 90° but less than 180°
4.	Straight angle		An angle measuring exactly 180°
5.	Reflex angle		An angle larger than 180° but less than 360°
6.	Complementary angles		Two angles whose sum is 90°
7.	Supplementary angles		Two angles whose sum is 180°
8.	Adjacent angles		Two angles that have a common side
9.	Vertical angles		The opposite angles that are formed when two lines intersect. Vertical angles are equal in measure.

LESSON

Defining Angles: Check for Understanding

Name: _____ Date: _____ Hr: _____

Directions: Eighteen angles or angle pairs are drawn in the boxes below. There are two examples of each term on the page "Defining Angles: Student Note Sheet." Identify each type of angle shown. You may use your note-taking sheet.

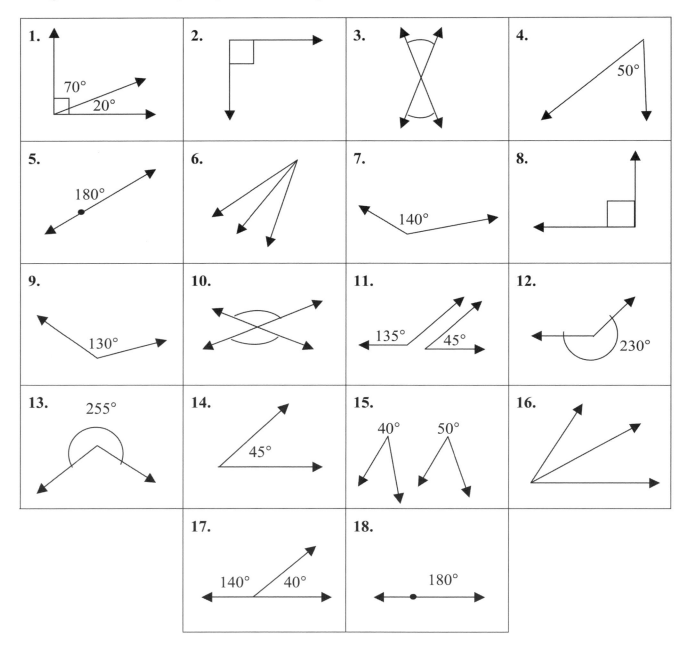

From *Making Math Accessible for the At-Risk Student: Grades 7–12* by Linda Ptacek. Santa Barbara, CA: Libraries Unlimited. Copyright © 2011.

LESSON

Defining Angles: Student Worksheet

Name: _____ Date: _____ Hr: _____

Directions: Examine the following diagram and name the angles listed below it. Lines AD and BH are parallel. Remember to use three points to name each angle in your answers. Ex: ∠FDC

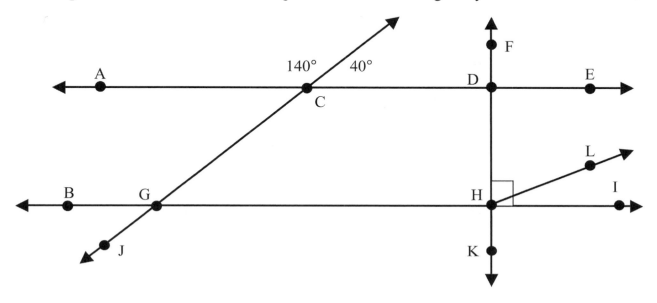

1. Name 2 acute angles: _____ and _____

2. Name 2 right angles: _____ and _____

3. Name 2 obtuse angles: _____ and _____

4. Name 2 straight angles: _____ and _____

5. Name 2 reflex angles: _____ and _____

6. Name a pair of complementary angles: _____ and _____

7. Name a pair of supplementary angles: _____ and _____

8. Name 2 adjacent angles: _____ and _____

9. Name a pair of vertical angles: _____ and _____

LESSON

Dog-Gone Awesome Math (DGAM): Teacher Page

Content: Solving multistep equations

Standard(s):

About This Activity . . .

Many students have difficulty remembering the process for solving multistep equations. For some of them, having a mnemonic device helps. This story has been written to illustrate the mnemonic DGAM (Dog-Gone Awesome Math). It follows two families, the Variables and the Constants, on their moving-day misadventures. For this activity, each student needs a copy of the story, a step-by-step explanation sheet, and a practice worksheet. Begin by reading the story aloud to the class, and then as a group work through the four-step process to solve the sample equation on the next page. Discuss each step of the process, and then as a group do several practice problems. Remind them that although not every problem has four steps, they still need to check to see if each step is necessary. If there is no need to distribute or to gather, just move on to the next step. Ask the students to finish the 12 problems on the worksheet on their own. Remind them to be very careful copying the problems to their own paper and to double-check that the problem is copied correctly before they begin to solve it. The worksheet solutions are listed at the bottom of the page, so the students can check their own work. If their solution does not match the one at the bottom, they should rework the problem.

Helpful reminders for students having difficulty solving equations: Copy the problem carefully. Write out each step moving <u>down</u> your page; do not write steps side-by-side. Draw a vertical line from the equal sign down into your workspace to help keep terms lined up. Circle your answer to make it easier to locate.

	Activity 6	
P	**A**	**G**

Name: _____ Date:_____ Hr:_____

Moving Day for the Variables and the Constants
(An Equation-Solving Tale)

It is moving day for the Variable and Constant families. These two families have been sharing a

storage unit while their new houses were being built, and it was a little too much togetherness!

Finally, their houses are done, and they are ready to move in, across the street from each other.

The Variables will live on the left side of the street; the Constants will live on the right side of

the street. For the last week they have been carefully packing and labeling all of their belongings.

As a cost-saving measure, they decided to have the neighborhood kids help them move all the

boxes. Big mistake! The boxes were quickly carried to the two houses, but some of each family's

boxes ended up in the other family's house. So now they have called a professional mover to

straighten things out, Dog-Gone Awesome Math Movers, owned by two former algebra teachers.

Dog-Gone Awesome Math (DGAM)

Name: _____ Date: _____ Hr: _____

The movers first draw a line down the middle of the street to show their work zones. Then they quickly split up and go to the two houses to reorganize the boxes. All the Variables go on the left, and all the Constants go on the right.

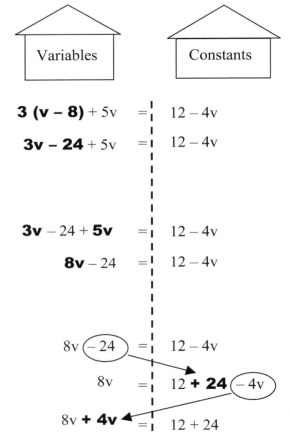

$3(v - 8) + 5v = 12 - 4v$

$3v - 24 + 5v = 12 - 4v$

Step 1: <u>DISTRIBUTE</u> to simplify the equation.

$3v - 24 + 5v = 12 - 4v$

$8v - 24 = 12 - 4v$

Step 2: <u>GATHER LIKE TERMS</u> on each side of the equation.

$8v \boxed{-24} = 12 - 4v$

$8v = 12 + 24 \boxed{-4v}$

$8v + 4v = 12 + 24$

$12v = 36$

Step 3: <u>ADDRESS IT</u>
One by one, move the terms with variables to the left side and the constants to the right side and combine them with what is already there. Think of the sign in front of each term as its address. Anytime you move a term from one side of the equal sign to the other, change its sign. For example, when the –24 on the left side moves to the right side, it becomes +24.

$$\frac{12v}{12} = \frac{36}{12}$$

$v = 3$

Step 4: <u>MAKE IT ONE</u>
Divide both sides of the equation by the number in front of the variable.

Always circle your answer, so you can find it easily!

LESSON

Dog-Gone Awesome Math (DGAM): Student Worksheet

	Activity 6	
P	**A**	**G**

Name: _____ Date: _____ Hr: _____

Dog-Gone Awesome Math Movers

.⸙DGAM.⸙

You always figure into our equation!

D = DISTRIBUTE

G = GATHER LIKE TERMS

A = ADDRESS IT

M = MAKE IT ONE

Directions: Solve each of the equations below on your own paper. Copy the problems carefully so you do not make mistakes. Just one sign makes a big difference! The answers to the problems are at the bottom of the page, so you can check yourself.
You must show your steps to get credit.

1. $9(d-4) = 27$	**2.** $3(6x-13) = -3$	**3.** $-(x-16) = 16$
4. $8 = 4(5c-8)$	**5.** $2(v+3) = 7v+36$	**6.** $-12(3-2k) = 108$
7. $-11w+45 = -(w+45)$	**8.** $24-2x = -4(3x-11)$	**9.** $9(7h+8) = 72+4h$
10. $6w-2(14-w) = w-21$	**11.** $4(x+9)+2x = 14-5x$	**12.** $8(x-3)+x = -48+x$

Check your solutions against the ones below. If you did not get the correct answer, make sure you copied the problem correctly and then rework the problem.

1. 7   **2.** 2   **3.** 0   **4.** 2   **5.** −6   **6.** 6   **7.** 9   **8.** 2   **9.** 0   **10.** 1   **11.** −2   **12.** −3

LESSON

Divisibility Rules: Teacher Page

Content: Divisibility rules

Standard(s):

About This Activity . . .

This partner activity is designed to reinforce divisibility rules. Each pair of students needs a spinner, and each student needs a "Divisibility Rules" handout and student worksheet. The spinners can be purchased or constructed from cardstock. Divide the spinner circle into eight sections, and label each section with the following integers: 2, 3, 4, 5, 6, 7, 9, 10. Before beginning the activity, ask each pair of students to take out a sheet of paper and number it from 1 to 10. Before the teacher reads the first question, ask the pairs to spin for a number and write it down next to #1 on their paper. Then the teacher reads Question #1 on the Teacher Question Page. The students write down the number underlined in the question and determine if it is divisible by the number they spun, noting it as YES or NO. When finished, the teacher can read the solutions listed below each question and have the students check their own work. Then have students complete the student worksheet. The worksheet answers are shown below.

Note: Remind students to save the "Divisibility Rules" handout in the "Tools" section of their notebook.

1. 428 is divisible by 2, 4

2. 224 is divisible by 2, 4, 7

3. 522 is divisible by 2, 3, 6, 9

4. 860 is divisible by 2, 4, 5, 10

5. 357 is divisible by 3, 7

6. 432 is divisible by 2, 3, 6, 9

7. 378 is divisible by 2, 3, 6, 7, 9

8. 120 is divisible by 2, 3, 4, 5, 6, 10

9. 351 is divisible by 3, 9

10. 720 is divisible by 2, 3, 4, 5, 6, 9, 10

11. 531 is divisible by 3, 9

12. 165 is divisible by 3, 5

STUDENT TOOL

Divisibility Rules

Name: _____ Date: _____ Hr: _____

How can you tell whether one number is divisible by another number
(leaving no remainder) without actually doing the division?

You can divide by …	If …
2	… the number is even (ends in a 0, 2, 4, 6, 8) Examples: 12, 334, 1006
3	… the sum of the digits is divisible by 3 Example: 1236 (1 + 2 + 3 + 6 = 12, and 12 is divisible by 3)
4	… the last two digits form a number divisible by 4 Examples: 124 (24 is divisible by 4), 5016 (16 is divisible by 4)
5	… the last digit is a 5 or a 0 Examples: 150, 2225
6	… it is even and the sum of its digits is divisible by 3 Example: 186 (1 + 8 + 6 = 15 and 15 is divisible by 3)
7	… when you double the last digit and subtract it from the rest of the number, you get 0 or a number divisible by 7 Example: 175 ($5 \times 2 = 10$ and $17 - 10 = 7$ and 7 is divisible by 7)
9	… the sum of the digits is divisible by 9 Example: 855 (8 + 5 + 5 = 18 and 18 is divisible by 9)
10	… the number ends in 0 Examples: 1400, 120

Prime numbers are divisible only by the number 1 and themselves.

What are the first 10 prime numbers? _2_, ___, ___, ___, ___, ___, ___, ___, ___, ___

Composite numbers have three or more numbers that divide into them.

From *Making Math Accessible for the At-Risk Student: Grades 7–12* by Linda Ptacek. Santa Barbara, CA: Libraries Unlimited. Copyright © 2011.

Divisibility Rules: Teacher Question Page and Solutions

1. There are <u>432</u> candy corns in a bag. Are they divisible by your number?

   Solution: **2, 3, 4, 6, 9**

2. There are <u>140</u> chairs in the cafeteria. Are they divisible by your number?

   Solution: **2, 4, 5, 7, 10**

3. A recipe makes <u>84</u> cookies. Are they divisible by your number?

   Solution: **2, 3, 4, 6, 7**

4. Sam's penny jar has <u>343</u> coins in it. Are they divisible by your number?

   Solution: **7**

5. There are <u>120</u> old CDs in the basement. Are they divisible by your number?

   Solution: **2, 3, 4, 5, 6, 10**

6. There are <u>243</u> fish in the aquarium. Are they divisible by your number?

   Solution: **3, 9**

7. I have <u>240</u> sheets of graph paper. Are they divisible by your number?

   Solution: **2, 3, 4, 5, 6, 10**

8. There are <u>210</u> chips in a bag. Are they divisible by your number?

   Solution: **2, 3, 5, 6, 7, 10**

9. There are <u>315</u> pretzels in a bag. Are they divisible by your number?

   Solution: **3, 5, 7, 9**

10. There are <u>840</u> cans of soda for the party. Are they divisible by your number?

    Solution: **2, 3, 4, 5, 6, 7, 10**

LESSON

Divisibility Rules: Student Worksheet

Name: _____ Date: _____ Hr: _____

Directions: Use the divisibility rules on each of the numbers in the left column. Put an X in the box of every number that divides evenly into them. **Note:** It will be easier to complete the chart up and down than left to right.

		2	3	4	5	6	7	9	10
1.	428								
2.	224								
3.	522								
4.	860								
5.	357								
6.	432								
7.	378								
8.	120								
9.	351								
10.	720								
11.	531								
12.	165								

Factoring Quadratic Trinomials: Teacher Pages

Content: Factoring simple quadratic trinomials

Standard(s):

About These Activities . . .

Activities 8–13 are worksheets that focus on the different steps of factoring basic quadratic trinomials. A brief description of each activity follows. Each of the handouts is intended to be an introduction to one of the steps, not a homework assignment. Additional practice problems will be needed at each step. Solutions for all worksheets follow Activity 13.

Activity 8: Step 1, Finding Pairs of Factors

In this activity, students are given 14 numbers for which they need to generate all the pairs of factors. The first factor of each pair is given. For students who cannot remember basic multiplication facts, this process is difficult. Show those students how to use the multiplication table to identify pairs of factors. Sometimes, in order to perform a more complex operation, they need a tool for one of the basic components. Students should save this completed worksheet to use on Activities 9–13.

Activity 9: Step 2, Sums and Differences of Factors

Using the factors generated in the previous activity, students are now asked to find factors with a specific sum or difference. These same numbers will be used in each of the following activities, so students can continue to focus on the new steps of the process instead of generating factors.

Activity 10: Step 3, What in the World Is a Quadratic Trinomial?

This activity reviews several basic terms: *constant, variable, coefficient, term,* and *like terms.* It also introduces the following new terms: *monomial, polynomial, binomial, trinomial,* and *quadratic trinomial.*

Activity 11: Step 4, Review of FOILing

In order for students to understand where they are going, it is often helpful for them to revisit a place they have been. In this case, since FOILing binomials is the inverse of factoring quadratic trinomials, it makes an excellent review. After practicing the FOIL process, explain that students will be doing the process in reverse for the next day's activity.

Activity 12: Step 5, Reading the Clues and Setting Up the Binomials

Students need to have a clear understanding of the relationship between the quadratic trinomial's signs and those of its resulting binomials. Will the binomial signs be the same or different? This is a difficult step for many students with disabilities, and it will require practice and repetition. Keep reminding them to "read from the back." It will also be helpful if you repeat the exact wording of your thought process with each problem. Before assigning the worksheet, call out the problem numbers and have the class respond with "same" or "different" to make sure they have the concept.

Activity 13: Step 6, Putting It All Together

This is where it becomes interesting and all the pieces should come together! For this step, emphasize why it was so important to practice finding factors with specific sums and differences. Then ask students to practice using all six steps to factor a series of quadratic trinomials. Remind them to use the factor sheet they completed in Activity 8 for this activity.

Factoring Quadratic Trinomials: Step 1

Name: _____ Date: _____ Hr: _____

Finding Pairs of Factors

Directions: Factors are integers that divide evenly into another number. Each factor has a partner. Each of the numbers in the left-hand column below has more than one pair of factors. Find the partner for each factor listed and fill in the blanks.

8	1 x _8_	2 x _4_	The factors of 8 are 1, 8, 2, and 4.			
12	1 x ____	2 x ____	3 x____			
16	1 x ____	2 x ____	4 x____			
18	1 x ____	2 x ____	3 x____			
24	1 x ____	2 x ____	3 x ____	4 x ____		
26	1 x ____	2 x ____				
32	1 x ____	2 x ____	4 x ____			
36	1 x ____	2 x ____	3 x ____	4 x ____	6 x ____	
40	1 x ____	2 x ____	4 x ____	5 x ____		
44	1 x ____	2 x ____	4 x ____			
45	1 x ____	3 x ____	5 x ____			
48	1 x ____	2 x ____	3 x ____	4 x ____	6 x ____	
54	1 x ____	2 x ____	3 x ____	6 x ____		
60	1 x ____	2 x ____	3 x ____	4 x ____	5 x ____	6 x ____

Multiplication Table

Name: _____ Date: _____ Hr: _____

TOOL

0	1	2	3	4	5	6	7	8	9	10	11	12	13	14	15	16	17	18	19	20
1	1	2	3	4	5	6	7	8	9	10	11	12	13	14	15	16	17	18	19	20
2	2	4	6	8	10	12	14	16	18	20	22	24	26	28	30	32	34	36	38	40
3	3	6	9	12	15	18	21	24	27	30	33	36	39	42	45	48	51	54	57	60
4	4	8	12	16	20	24	28	32	36	40	44	48	52	56	60	64	68	72	76	80
5	5	10	15	20	25	30	35	40	45	50	55	60	65	70	75	80	85	90	95	100
6	6	12	18	24	30	36	42	48	54	60	66	72	78	84	90	96	102	108	114	120
7	7	14	21	28	35	42	49	56	63	70	77	84	91	98	105	112	119	126	133	140
8	8	16	24	32	40	48	56	64	72	80	88	96	104	112	120	128	136	144	152	160
9	9	18	27	36	45	54	63	72	81	90	99	108	117	126	135	144	153	162	171	180
10	10	20	30	40	50	60	70	80	90	100	110	120	130	140	150	160	170	180	190	200
11	11	22	33	44	55	66	77	88	99	110	121	132	143	154	165	176	187	198	209	220
12	12	24	36	48	60	72	84	96	108	120	132	144	156	168	180	192	204	216	228	240
13	13	26	39	52	65	78	91	104	117	130	143	156	169	182	195	208	221	234	247	260
14	14	28	42	56	70	84	98	112	126	140	154	168	182	196	210	224	238	252	266	280
15	15	30	45	60	75	90	105	120	135	150	165	180	195	210	225	240	255	270	285	300

Factoring Quadratic Trinomials: Step 2

Name: _____ Date: _____ Hr: _____

Sums and Differences of Factors

Directions: Use the information from your completed "Finding Pairs of Factors" worksheet to fill in the grid below. You will be finding pairs of factors that have a given sum or difference.

Find the factors of:	With a sum of:	Your answer ↓↓↓	With a difference of:	Your answer ↓↓↓
8	9	8 and 1	2	4 and 2
12	13		1	
16	10		6	
18	9		7	
24	11		23	
26	27		11	
32	12		14	
36	13		16	
40	13		6	
44	15		43	
45	18		4	
48	19		2	
54	15		25	
60	17		11	

Factoring Quadratic Trinomials: Step 3

Name: _____ Date: _____ Hr: _____

What in the World Is a Quadratic Trinomial?

Part A: A quick review …

What is a constant?		Circle the constants:
A constant is a number that does not change.	3 17 −28 $\frac{1}{2}$ .236 are all constants.	2 xy $\frac{1}{4}$ −9 h .7 102
What is a variable?		Circle the variables:
A variable is a letter that "stands in" for a number. It is a quantity that can change. Any letter can be a variable.	$2\mathbf{x} + 7$ $4\mathbf{a} = 32$ $5\mathbf{abc}$	2 xy $\frac{1}{4}$ 94 14rs −11 7b
What is a coefficient?		Circle the coefficient of x in each term below:
A coefficient is the number that is in front of a variable or string of variables.	$\mathbf{4}x$ $\mathbf{-8}xyz$	−2x $\frac{1}{4}$ x 15x 22x $-\frac{1}{2}$ x
What is a term?	Each of these is a term:	Circle the terms:
A term can be a variable, a constant, or a multiplied variable-constant combination.	x 13 xy^2 −6h These are **not** terms: 13x + 2y and x − 7	12y 152 x + 6 −4x + y −4xy
What are like terms?	These are **like** terms:	Circle the like terms:
Like terms have the same variable(s) to the same power(s).	4x and −3x These are **unlike** terms: 4x and $4x^2$	4y −6y 4x $7y^2$ Write a pair of like terms: _____ and _____

From *Making Math Accessible for the At-Risk Student: Grades 7–12* by Linda Ptacek. Santa Barbara, CA: Libraries Unlimited. Copyright © 2011.

58

Part B: Now for the new pieces!

What is a monomial? A monomial is an algebraic expression with only one term. It can be a variable, a constant, or a multiplied variable-constant combination.	Each of these is a monomial: x 13 xy −6h	Circle the monomials: x + 6 2y 15x
What is a polynomial? A polynomial is an algebraic expression with more than one term linked by addition or subtraction. Some polynomials have special names (binomial and trinomial).	Each of these is a polynomial: 2x − 6 (2 terms) 7r − 4s + 2t (3 terms) 7r − 4s + 2t − 9 (4 terms)	Write a polynomial with 5 terms:
What is a binomial? A binomial is an algebraic expression with two terms linked by addition or subtraction.	Each of these is a binomial: x + 13 and −6h − 5	Circle the binomials: x + 6 2y 15x − 8
What is a trinomial? A trinomial is an algebraic expression with three terms linked by addition or subtraction.	This is a trinomial: 7x + 2y − 3z	Circle the trinomials: x + y − 6 2xyz 15a − b + c
What is a quadratic trinomial? A quadratic trinomial is a three-term expression whose highest exponent is 2. Terms are usually written in descending order of exponents.	This is a quadratic trinomial $3x^2 − 2x + 7$ ↓ ↓ ↓ x^2 x^1 x^0 (descending order of exponents)	Write these quadratic trinomials in descending order of exponents: $−7x + 5x^2 + 8$ $−14 + 9x + 2x^2$

Factoring Quadratic Trinomials: Step 4

Name: _____ Date: _____ Hr: _____

Review of FOILing

To understand factoring quadratic trinomials, sometimes it helps to work backwards and see where quadratic trinomials come from. This worksheet reviews FOILing, a way to multiply binomials. Two binomials are shown below. With the FOIL process, each term in the first binomial gets multiplied by each term in the second binomial.

$$(x + 3) \ (x - 5)$$

Multiply the **F**irst terms of each one together.	**F**	$(\mathbf{x} + 3) \ (\mathbf{x} - 5)$ .... x^2
Next multiply the **O**utside terms together.	**O**	$(\mathbf{x} + 3) \ (x - \mathbf{5})$ .... $-5x$
Third, multiply the **I**nside terms,	**I**	$(x + \mathbf{3}) \ (\mathbf{x} - 5)$ ....$+3x$
And, finally, multiply the **L**ast terms.	**L**	$(x + \mathbf{3}) \ (x - \mathbf{5})$ .... -15

After you complete the four steps of the FOIL process, gather your four products, combine any like terms, and you have your answer!

$$x^2 \underline{- 5x} \underline{+ 3x} - 15$$
$$\downarrow \quad \downarrow$$
combine

The quadratic trinomial $x^2 - 2x - 15$ is your answer.

Practice FOILing these three pairs of binomials. The answers are given at the bottom of each problem so you can check yourself. Please show all of your work.

Sample 1: $(x + 5) \ (x + 3)$ Sample 2: $(n - 7) \ (n + 8)$ Sample 3: $(c - 1) \ (c - 6)$

Answer: $x^2 + 8x + 15$ Answer: $n^2 + n - 56$ Answer: $c^2 - 7c + 6$

Factoring Quadratic Trinomials: Step 4

Name: _____ Date: _____ Hr: _____

Directions: Use the FOIL method to multiply each pair of binomials below. Show your steps.

1. $(b + 2)(b + 5)$	**2.** $(c + 3)(c - 6)$	**3.** $(d - 8)(d + 4)$
4. $(h - 9)(h - 7)$	**5.** $(b + 2)(b + 3)$	**6.** $(c + 4)(c - 5)$
7. $(d - 6)(d + 7)$	**8.** $(h - 8)(h - 9)$	**9.** $(b + 2)(b + 9)$
10. $(c + 3)(c - 8)$	**11.** $(d - 4)(d + 7)$	**12.** $(h - 5)(h - 6)$

Factoring Quadratic Trinomials: Step 5

Name: _____ Date: _____ Hr: _____

Reading the Clues and Setting Up the Binomials

Factoring quadratic trinomials is the reverse of FOILing. You start with a trinomial and back up until you have a pair of binomials. There are signs to read along the way to help you decide what to do next. Every quadratic trinomial has two signs, a front sign and a back sign, and those signs tell you everything you need to know about setting up your binomial factors.

$$x^2 + 10x + 16 \quad \leftarrow \text{Start at the back and read to the left.}$$

$x^2 + 10x \,(\mathbf{+})\, 16$	$x^2 \,(\mathbf{+})\, 10x + 16$
The back sign tells you if the binomials will have the same signs or different signs. Plus means "same" and minus means "different."	If the signs are to be the same, the first sign of the trinomial lets you know if they will both be plus or both be minus.

$x^2 + 10x + 16$ The binomial factors of this trinomial will have the same signs.

They will both be plus. $(x +)(x +)$

$x^2 - 15x + 44$ The binomial factors of this trinomial will have the same signs.

They will both be minus. $(x -)(x -)$

$x^2 + 6x - 16$ The binomial factors of this trinomial will have different signs.

Note: Each binomial has to start with an x to produce the x^2 in the trinomial.

Example 1: $x^2 + 6x + 8$	Signs will be the same. +	$(x + \quad)(x + \quad)$
Circle the sign in the trinomial that tells you both binomials will have + signs.		
Example 2: $x^2 - 15x + 44$	Signs will be the same. −	$(x - \quad)(x - \quad)$
Circle the sign in the trinomial that tells you both binomials will have − signs.		
Example 3: $x^2 + 6x - 16$	Signs will be different.	$(x + \quad)(x - \quad)$
Circle the sign in the trinomial that tells you the binomials' signs will be different.		

Factoring Quadratic Trinomials: Step 5

Name: _____ Date: _____ Hr: _____

Directions: Look at each quadratic trinomial below. Read its clues from back to front. Then fill in the signs for its binomial factors. The first three have been done for you as examples.

1.	$x^2 + 9x + 8$	$(x + \quad)(x + \quad)$
2.	$x^2 - 15x + 44$	$(x - \quad)(x - \quad)$
3.	$x^2 + 6x - 16$	$(x + \quad)(x - \quad)$
4.	$x^2 - 23x - 24$	$(x \quad)(x \quad)$
5.	$x^2 - 11x - 26$	$(x \quad)(x \quad)$
6.	$x^2 + 6x - 40$	$(x \quad)(x \quad)$
7.	$x^2 + 19x + 48$	$(x \quad)(x \quad)$
8.	$x^2 - 17x + 60$	$(x \quad)(x \quad)$
9.	$x^2 - 9x + 18$	$(x \quad)(x \quad)$
10.	$x^2 + 1x - 12$	$(x \quad)(x \quad)$
11.	$x^2 + 15x + 54$	$(x \quad)(x \quad)$
12.	$x^2 + 14x - 32$	$(x \quad)(x \quad)$
13.	$x^2 - 15x + 36$	$(x \quad)(x \quad)$
14.	$x^2 - 12x - 45$	$(x \quad)(x \quad)$
15.	$x^2 + 12x + 32$	$(x \quad)(x \quad)$
16.	$x^2 + 2x - 48$	$(x \quad)(x \quad)$
17.	$x^2 - 8x + 16$	$(x \quad)(x \quad)$
18.	$x^2 - 20x - 44$	$(x \quad)(x \quad)$

Factoring Quadratic Trinomials: Step 6

Activity 13		
P	**A**	**G**

Name: _____ Date: _____ Hr: _____

Putting It All Together: Once you understand factors and the sign placement in the binomials, the last step in factoring trinomials is easy. Let's use $x^2 - 15x + 44$ as an example. You know that the signs in the binomial factors will both be the same and they will both be minus. Once again, reading the trinomial from back to front ask yourself, "What two factors of 44 add together to get 15?" The answer: 11 and 4. Your binomial factors are $(x - 11)(x - 4)$.

$x^2 + \boxed{11x + 24}$ What two factors of 24 add together to get 11? (8 and 3)

$x^2 + \boxed{16x - 36}$ What two factors of 36 subtract to get 16? (2 and 18)

$x^2 - \boxed{2x - 48}$ What two factors of 48 subtract to get 2? (6 and 8)

Directions: Factor the trinomials listed in the first column below. If both binomials have the same sign, it does not matter which factor goes in which binomial. If the signs in the binomial are different, the larger factor's sign must match the front sign in the trinomial.

1.	$x^2 + 9x + 8$	What 2 factors of 8 add up to 9?	(x +) (x +)
2.	$x^2 - 15x + 44$	What 2 factors of 44 add up to 15?	(x −) (x −)
3.	$x^2 + 6x - 16$	What 2 factors of 16 subtract to get 6?	(x +) (x −)
4.	$x^2 - 23x - 24$	What 2 factors of 24 subtract to get 23?	(x) (x)
5.	$x^2 - 11x - 26$	What 2 factors of 26 subtract to get 11?	(x) (x)
6.	$x^2 + 6x - 40$	What 2 factors of 40 subtract to get 6?	(x) (x)
7.	$x^2 + 19x + 48$	What 2 factors of 48 add up to 19?	(x) (x)
8.	$x^2 - 17x + 60$	What 2 factors of 60 add up to 17?	(x) (x)
9.	$x^2 - 9x + 18$	What 2 factors of 18 add up to 9?	(x) (x)
10.	$x^2 + 1x - 12$	What 2 factors of 12 subtract to get 1?	(x) (x)

Activities 8–13: **Factoring Quadratic Trinomials**: Solutions

P
A
G

Activity 13
1. $(x+8)(x+1)$
2. $(x-11)(x-4)$
3. $(x+8)(x-2)$
4. $(x-24)(x+1)$
5. $(x-13)(x+2)$
6. $(x-4)(x+10)$
7. $(x+16)(x+3)$
8. $(x-12)(x-5)$
9. $(x-6)(x-3)$
10. $(x+4)(x-3)$

Activity 12
1. $(\ +\ )(\ +\ )$
2. $(\ -\ )(\ -\ )$
3. $(\ +\ )(\ -\ )$
4. $(\ +\ )(\ -\ )$
5. $(\ +\ )(\ -\ )$
6. $(\ +\ )(\ -\ )$
7. $(\ +\ )(\ +\ )$
8. $(\ -\ )(\ -\ )$
9. $(\ -\ )(\ -\ )$
10. $(\ +\ )(\ -\ )$
11. $(\ +\ )(\ +\ )$
12. $(\ +\ )(\ -\ )$
13. $(\ -\ )(\ -\ )$
14. $(\ +\ )(\ -\ )$
15. $(\ +\ )(\ +\ )$
16. $(\ +\ )(\ -\ )$
17. $(\ -\ )(\ -\ )$
18. $(\ +\ )(\ -\ )$

Activity 11
1. $b^2+7b+10$
2. $c^2-3c-18$
3. $d^2-4d-32$
4. $h^2-16h+63$
5. b^2+5b+6
6. c^2-c-20
7. d^2+d-42
8. $h^2-17h+72$
9. $b^2+11b+18$
10. $c^2-5c-24$
11. $d^2+3d-28$
12. $h^2-11h+30$

Activity 12
Examples
1. $(x+4)(x+2)$
2. $(x-11)(x-4)$
3. $(x+8)(x-2)$

Activity 10
Constants:
$2 \quad \frac{1}{4} \quad -9 \quad .7 \quad 102$

Variables:
$xy \quad rs \quad b$

Coefficients:
$-2\frac{1}{4} \quad 15 \quad 22 \quad -\frac{1}{2}$

Terms:
$12y \quad 152 \quad -4xy$

Like terms:
$4y$ and $-6y$

Monomials:
$2y$ and $15x$

Polynomial:
Answers will vary

Binomials:
$x+6$ and $15x-8$

Trinomials:
$x+y-6$
$15a-b+c$

Descending order:
$5x^2-7x+8$
$2x^2+9x-14$

Activity 9
Factors of ...

8...8,1 4,2
12...12,1 4,3
16...8,2 8,2
18...3,6 9,2
24...3,8 24,1
26...26,1 13,2
32...4,8 16,2
36...9,4 18,2
40...5,8 10,4
44...4,11 44,1
45...3,15 9,5
48...3,16 8,6
54...6,9 27,2
60...5,12 15,4

Activity 8
Factors of ...

8...8,4
12...6,4
16...8,4
18...9,6
24...12,8,6
26...13
32...16,8
36...18,12,9,6
40...20,10,8
44...22,11
45...15,9
48...24,16,12,8
54...27,18,9
60...30,20,15,12,10

Alpha Math: Student Handout

Name: _____ Date: _____ Hr: _____

You will earn one point for each math word you put into the grid below. You may not use more than one variation of a word: subtract (yes), subtraction, subtracted, subtracting (no). The only number you may use is ZERO (There's your Z word!).

Addition	A	A
Bar graph	B	B
Calculate	C	C
D	D	D
E	E	E
F	F	F
G	G	G
H	H	H
I	I	I
J	J	J
K	K	K
L	L	L
M	M	M
N	N	N
O	O	O
P	P	P
Q	Q	Q
R	R	R
S	S	S
T	T	T
U	U	U
V	V	V
W	W	W
X	X	X
Y	Y	Y
Z	Z	Z

FIRST WEEK

Find the Sign: Student Handout

Name: _____ Date: _____ Hr: _____

In math, we use symbols as a shortcut way of writing commonly used operations and words. In the shaded boxes, use symbols, letters, and numbers to translate the words to the right. Questions 1–10 deal with basic algebra, and questions 11–20 deal with geometry.

1.		a number "n" squared	**11.**		angle ABC
2.		the absolute value of negative nine	**12.**		triangle DEF
3.		b is greater than or equal to c	**13.**		pi
4.		c is not equal to d	**14.**		is similar to
5.		infinity	**15.**		line CD
6.		negative seventeen	**16.**		lines r and s are parallel
7.		parentheses	**17.**		segment QR is perpendicular to segment ST
8.		r plus or minus four	**18.**		ray EF
9.		the square root of sixteen	**19.**		right angle
10.		twenty percent	**20.**		thirty-two degrees

FIRST WEEK

Hello, My Name Is ...

Name: _____ Date: _____ Hr: _____

Address: _____

Home Phone Number: _____

Parent(s) Work Phone Number(s): _____

Parent(s) E-mail: _____

1. List the names and ages of the people who live at your house and their relationship to you.

_____

_____

2. How do you get to and from school? _____

3. Where do you usually do your homework ? _____

4. What is your best math skill? _____

5. What is one thing you never really understood last year in math class?

_____

6. On a scale of 1–5, how hard is math for you?   1   2   3   4   5

(Circle a number. 1 means "very easy," and 5 means "very hard.")

7. What can teachers do to make it easier for you to learn? _____

_____

8. What is your favorite way to work?   solo   with a partner   in a group

9. What is your best subject? _____ Worst? _____

10. What do you like to do in your free time away from school? _____

_____

11. What clubs, sports, or extracurricular activities do you participate in OR

would you like to learn more about? _____

_____

12. What are your plans after high school? _____

_____

13. What is your biggest worry as you start this new school year? _____

_____

14. What is something you want to accomplish this year either in school or outside

of school? _____

15. What do your friends like best about you? _____

_____

16. What has been the proudest moment in your life to this point? _____

_____

_____

17. What three words best describe you?

_____   _____   _____

18. If you have trouble with your math homework, who usually helps you?

_____

_____

Info Circles: Teacher Page

About This Activity . . .

To prepare for this activity, make 11 wall posters, each one with a large circle and one of the "getting-to-know-you" questions indicated on the following page. Divide the circles into sections based on the number of possible answers for that question. Display these posters around the classroom. Divide the students into 11 equal groups and send each group to a different poster. Allow one minute for them to sign their full names (only once) in the appropriate section of the circle, then call out, "Rotate." Each group of students should then move clockwise to the next poster. When you have finished, leave the posters up for a week or two, so students can get to know each other a little better. The information you gather in this activity can also be saved for later in the year to put into graphs and charts. An example of poster question 11 is shown below.

Example Poster:

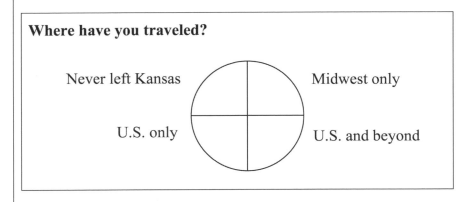

Where have you traveled?

Never left Kansas   Midwest only

U.S. only   U.S. and beyond

1. **How many people live in your house?**

   2   3–4   5–6   More than 6

2. **What is your favorite type of movie?**

   Comedy   Action-Adventure   Romance   Sci-Fi   Horror

3. **What are your plans after high school?**

   College   Job   Military   Other   Undecided

4. **If you won a free trip, where would you go?**

   Mountains   Beach   New York   Disneyland   Cruise

5. **What is your favorite type of music?**

   Pop   Country   Rap   Christian   Alternative   Other

6. **How many hours of sleep do you get on a school night?**

   Less than 6   6   7   8   More than 8

7. **Which vehicle would you rather have?**

   Sports Car   Pickup Truck   Jeep   Motorcycle

8. **What is your favorite fast food?**

   Pizza   Burger   Taco   Chicken   Sub Sandwich

9. **Which do you prefer?**

   Movies   Music   Shopping   Sports   Computer

10. **Where do you spend the most money?**

    Clothes   Car   Food   Music   Gas   Other

11. **Where have you traveled?**

    Never left Kansas   Midwest only   U.S. only   U.S. and beyond

Key In to This: Teacher Page

Content: Calculator proficiency

Standard(s):

About This Activity . . .

For this activity, each student must have a scientific calculator in hand. It is not necessary, and in fact it is often more confusing for students to have a graphing calculator at the pre-algebra and algebra levels. It is important that they have the calculator they plan to use during the school year instead of a borrowed one, as they will be reviewing that calculator's functions. Since students may have a variety of different calculators, discuss each function individually as you circulate the room, making sure students are locating the correct keys on their calculators. When all the function keys have been identified and drawn in the second column of the handout, have the students "key in" the calculations. Give individual help to students who do not arrive at the correct answers. After the activity has been completed, ask the students to write "SAVE" in bold letters at the top of the sheet and keep it to use as a reference sheet throughout the year.

Solutions:

1. $\dfrac{37}{312}$ 2. -178 3. 9409   4. 46   5. .048

6. 49.6   7. 64   8. $\sqrt{}$ 9. $105\dfrac{17}{24}$

FIRST WEEK

Key In to This: Calculator Proficiency Student Handout

Name: _____ Date: _____ Hr: _____

Which calculator key is used to perform each of the following functions? Sketch the calculator key in Column 2 to the right of each function. When you have finished, then do each of the calculations in Column 3.

	The Functions:	**The Keys:**	**Key In:**	**Your Answer:**
1.	Input a fraction		$\frac{1}{13} + \frac{1}{24} =$	
2.	Input a negative number		$-267 - (-89) =$	
3.	Square a number		97 squared =	
4.	Calculate the square root of a number		Square root of 2,116 =	
5.	Convert a fraction to a decimal		$\frac{6}{125} =$	
6.	Input the value pi		Multiply pi by 15.8 = (Give answer to nearest tenth)	
7.	Calculate any number to a power greater than 2		4 to the 3rd power =	
8.	Access the second available function of any key		The second function of the "squared" key is …	
9.	Get the answer to your calculations		$\frac{1}{8} + 7.2 * 15 - 2\frac{5}{12} =$	
10.	Erase the last digit of your current entry			
11.	Turn off your calculator			

Skills Survey: Teacher Page

Content: Survey of basic pre-algebra skills

Standard(s):

About This Activity . . .

This two-page survey covers a range of topics from computation with whole numbers, decimals, integers, and fractions to solving equations. Allow students one class period to complete the activity. Use it as an indicator of which prerequisite skills they need to review or which skills need to be retaught prior to introducing new concepts. Remind students to work through the problems horizontally, not column by column. That will keep similar problem types together. Allow students to write answers directly on the survey. After you grade and record these tests, show them to the students, so they can see how they did. Then file the tests until the end of the year when you can retest and have students check their progress. Calculators may be used.

<u>Note:</u> Solutions to the Skills Survey are on the page following the test.

FIRST WEEK

Skills Survey: Student Handout

Name: _____ Date: _____ Hr: _____

Directions: Answer each question in the space provided. You MAY use a calculator.

1. $21 + 102 =$ **2.** $730 - 42 =$ **3.** $8 \times 112 =$ **4.** $497 \div 7 =$

5. $2.1 + 1.02 =$ **6.** $.730 - .42 =$ **7.** $.8 \times 1.12 =$ **8.** $4.97 \div .7 =$

9. $21 + (-102) =$ **10.** $730 - (-42) =$ **11.** $-8 \times 112 =$ **12.** $497 \div (-7) =$

13. $\frac{2}{3} + \frac{1}{5} =$ **14.** $\frac{3}{8} - \frac{1}{4} =$ **15.** $\frac{1}{2} \times \frac{3}{7} =$ **16.** $1\frac{3}{4} \div \frac{3}{8} =$

17. Evaluate: x^3 when $x = 4$ **18.** Evaluate: $8 \times (2 + 3)$ **19.** Evaluate: $(8 \times 2) + 3$ **20.** Reduce $\frac{21}{28}$ to lowest terms

21. Change .36 to a fraction in lowest terms. **22.** Change $\frac{7}{8}$ to a decimal. **23.** Change .28 to a percentage. **24.** Calculate 17π to the nearest tenth.

25. Write $4\frac{2}{7}$ as an improper fraction. **26.** Change 60% to a decimal. **27.** Write $\frac{12}{7}$ as a mixed number. **28.** Change $\frac{2}{5}$ to a percentage.

29. Write 2,051 in scientific notation.

30. Order from smallest to largest:

    –3   –5   –2.6

31. Find the mean of the following numbers:

    3, 8, 4, 8, 2

32. Find the median of the following numbers:

    2, 8, 4, 8, 2

33. Find the mode of the following numbers:

    23, 8, 14, 8, 22

34. Find the range of the following numbers:

    2, 8, 4, 8, 2

35. Find the next number in this sequence:

    2, 4, 8, 16, __

36. Use $A = \frac{1}{2} bh$ to find the area of this triangle.

37. Compare with < > or =

    $\frac{4}{7}$ $\frac{6}{10}$

38. Compare with < > or =

    .701   .82

39. Simplify this expression:

    $9x + 4 - 7x$

40. Round 4.0782 to the nearest hundredth.

41. Is (x)(x) equal to 2x or x^2?

42. Solve:
    $5x - 11 = 54$

43. Solve:
    $4x = 44$

44. Solve:
    $2x - 8 = 30$

45. Solve:
    $\frac{x}{7} = 5$

46. Write "four and eight thousandths" as a decimal.

47. Which fraction equals $\frac{1}{5}$?

    $\frac{1}{7}$ $\frac{2}{6}$ $\frac{3}{15}$

48. What is 4% of 18?

49. Simplify:
    $2(6x - 3)$

50. From the symbols at the right, what is P(♠)?

    ♣ ♣ ♣ ♣

    ♦ ♦

    ♥ ♥ ♥

    ♠

Skills Survey: Solutions

	Activity 19	
P	A	G

Solutions to Front Side of Skills Survey

1.	123	**2.**	688	**3.**	896	**4.**	71
5.	3.12	**6.**	.31	**7.**	.896	**8.**	7.1
9.	-81	**10.**	772	**11.**	-896	**12.**	-71
13.	$\frac{13}{15}$	**14.**	$\frac{1}{8}$	**15.**	$\frac{3}{14}$	**16.**	$\frac{14}{3}$
17.	64	**18.**	40	**19.**	19	**20.**	$\frac{3}{4}$
21.	$\frac{9}{25}$	**22.**	.875	**23.**	28%	**24.**	53.4
25.	$\frac{30}{7}$	**26.**	.6	**27.**	$1\frac{5}{7}$	**28.**	40%

Solutions to Back Side of Skills Survey

29.	2.051×10^3	**30.**	$-5, -3, -2.6$	**31.**	5	**32.**	4
33.	8	**34.**	6	**35.**	32	**36.**	14
37.	$<$	**38.**	$<$	**39.**	$2x + 4$	**40.**	4.08
41.	x^2	**42.**	13	**43.**	11	**44.**	19
45.	35	**46.**	4.008	**47.**	$\frac{3}{15}$	**48.**	.72
49.	$12x - 6$	**50.**	$\frac{1}{10}$				

LESSON

Fraction Interaction Part 1: Teacher Page

Content: Comparing fractions

Standard(s):

<table>
<tr><td colspan="3">**Activity 20**</td></tr>
<tr><td>P</td><td>A</td><td>G</td></tr>
</table>

About this activity . . .

Remind students that in mathematics there are often several ways to arrive at the right answer. Problem solving is like going on a road trip. Some people like to take the scenic route, some take the quickest route, and others like a more challenging route. For today's activity, you will be demonstrating four different ways to compare fractions, but the focus will be on the shortcut! Using the fractions $\frac{3}{4}$ and $\frac{4}{5}$ show the students how to compare the fractions by:

- making a graphic representation of each fraction with shaded squares.

- converting both fractions to new fractions with a common denominator.

- converting each fraction to a decimal.

- cross multiplying the fractions.

When demonstrating the cross multiplication method, use arrows to show which numbers to multiply and where to place the product for comparison purposes. There is an example at the top of the students' worksheet to remind them of the process. After finishing the four methods, discuss the advantages and disadvantages of each one with the students, and then use the cross multiplication method to complete the 12 "check for understanding" problems on the next page.

Solutions to Check for Understanding Problems:

1. =	2. <	3. <	4. =	5. >	6. <
7. >	8. <	9. =	10. >	11. <	12. =

LESSON

Fraction Interaction: Check for Understanding

	Activity 20	
P	**A**	**G**

Name: _____ Date:_____ Hr:_____

Example: $\dfrac{4}{6} \diagdown \dfrac{7}{10}$

$40 < 42$

To compare two fractions, cross multiply and then compare the products.

Directions: Compare each pair of fractions below using cross multiplication, then insert the correct sign between them. You must show your cross-products to get credit.

less than <   greater than >   equal to =

The first one has been done for you.

1. $\dfrac{6}{7} \diagup\diagdown \dfrac{18}{21}$ $126 = 126$	**2.** $\dfrac{4}{11} \qquad \dfrac{8}{21}$	**3.** $\dfrac{6}{7} \qquad \dfrac{7}{8}$
4. $\dfrac{2}{7} \qquad \dfrac{18}{63}$	**5.** $\dfrac{3}{5} \qquad \dfrac{1}{2}$	**6.** $\dfrac{6}{11} \qquad \dfrac{8}{13}$
7. $\dfrac{1}{7} \qquad \dfrac{5}{45}$	**8.** $\dfrac{2}{13} \qquad \dfrac{3}{14}$	**9.** $\dfrac{5}{6} \qquad \dfrac{35}{42}$
10. $\dfrac{5}{6} \qquad \dfrac{8}{10}$	**11.** $\dfrac{7}{11} \qquad \dfrac{4}{6}$	**12.** $\dfrac{3}{7} \qquad \dfrac{15}{35}$

Fraction Interaction Part 2: Teacher Page

Activity 20		
P	**A**	**G**

Content: Comparing fractions

Standard(s):

About this activity . . .

For this activity, students need to be arranged in groups of three, seated side-by-side and facing the front of the room. Before beginning the game, give each group of students three blank sheets of paper on which they should write the following information in large letters. Each student should then keep one of the sheets for the entire activity. It will be his job to raise that paper when the group determines which sign indicates the correct answer.

Greater than	**Less than**	**Equal to**
>	**<**	**=**

Explain to the class that for this activity, they will be shown pairs of fractions and must decide whether the first fraction is greater than, less than, or equal to the second fraction. When the teacher calls "Signs up!" the student holding the correct sign will raise it up. Groups will earn one point for each correct answer. The teacher should use the pairs of fractions on the student worksheet that follows. The worksheet can then also be assigned as homework.

Solutions to Student Worksheet Problems:

1. <	2. =	3. <	4. <	5. <	6. <
7. =	8. >	9. =	10. <	11. >	12. <
13. =	14. >	15. <	16. =	17. >	18. <
19. =	20. >	21. <			

Fraction Interaction: Student Worksheet

Name: _____ Date:_____ Hr:_____

Directions: Cross multiply to compare each pair of fractions below, then insert the correct sign
between them: **less than <**   **greater than >**   **equal to =**

1.	$\frac{2}{3}$	$\frac{4}{5}$	**2.**	$\frac{2}{5}$	$\frac{24}{60}$	**3.**	$\frac{3}{8}$	$\frac{5}{13}$
4.	$\frac{4}{6}$	$\frac{8}{10}$	**5.**	$\frac{2}{10}$	$\frac{4}{15}$	**6.**	$\frac{5}{6}$	$\frac{7}{8}$
7.	$\frac{2}{8}$	$\frac{10}{40}$	**8.**	$\frac{4}{8}$	$\frac{5}{11}$	**9.**	$\frac{6}{15}$	$\frac{2}{5}$
10.	$\frac{6}{11}$	$\frac{5}{9}$	**11.**	$\frac{2}{6}$	$\frac{4}{14}$	**12.**	$\frac{3}{7}$	$\frac{5}{9}$
13.	$\frac{7}{2}$	$\frac{42}{12}$	**14.**	$\frac{6}{7}$	$\frac{5}{6}$	**15.**	$\frac{6}{9}$	$\frac{12}{15}$
16.	$\frac{3}{4}$	$\frac{24}{32}$	**17.**	$\frac{3}{12}$	$\frac{1}{6}$	**18.**	$\frac{2}{13}$	$\frac{4}{15}$
19.	$\frac{2}{12}$	$\frac{4}{24}$	**20.**	$\frac{1}{3}$	$\frac{5}{20}$	**21.**	$\frac{2}{5}$	$\frac{5}{12}$

LESSON

Combining Like Terms: Teacher Page

Content: Introduction to combining like terms

Standard(s):

About This Activity . . . Ask students to pair up, moving their desks next to each other. Give one copy of the "Garage Sale" handout to each pair of students. Explain that the purpose of this garage sale activity is to discuss ways to categorize items, and that in the end it will tie into today's topic: combining like terms. Give several minutes for the partners to examine and discuss the garage sale problem. Then, as a class, brainstorm ways to organize the items and write those options on the board. As a group develop sub-categories for <u>one</u> of the options. Remind them that every item must logically fit into one of the categories they have outlined. Teams should then pick an organization system to use and outline their sub-categories. After they list and number the categories, they should then put the appropriate category number in front of each garage sale item. When all pairs have finished, conduct a class discussion about the methods of organization they used. Did all of their items clearly fit into one category and not the others? Finally, link this to today's topic using the "Combining Like Terms Graphic Organizer" to explain how algebraic terms are grouped. Then assign the student worksheet to be done individually.	**Student Worksheet Solutions** 1. unlike, different variables 2. like, same variables to same powers 3. unlike, different variables 4. unlike, different powers 5. like, same variables to same powers 6. $12v$ 7. $5w$ 8. cannot be combined. 9. $5h^2 + 10h$ 10. $10b - 7$ 11. $6x + 4y + 9$ 12. $y^2 + 4y + 3$

Combining Like Terms

Name: _____ Date:_____ Hr:_____

$\left(\text{G}\right)\left(\text{A}\right)\left(\text{R}\right)\left(\text{A}\right)\left(\text{G}\right)\left(\text{E}\right)$ $\left(\text{S}\right)\left(\text{A}\right)\left(\text{L}\right)\left(\text{E}\right)$

The Moyer family wants to have a garage sale. All of their friends tell them that garage sales that are well organized make the most money. Items have to be grouped together correctly to sell. They cannot agree on how the items should be organized. Can you help them?

_____ Stuffed animals	How would you group these items?
_____ Kids' clothes	By function? By size? By cost?
_____ Pots and pans	By who uses them?
_____ Toys, puzzles, and games	Decide on your method of grouping and then
_____ CDs and DVDs	develop several sub-categories and write them on
_____ Purses	the lines below. Number them.
_____ Christmas decorations	Then put one of the category numbers in front of
_____ Bikes and tricycles	each item at the garage sale.
_____ Jewelry	
_____ TV and DVD player	
_____ Adult coats	
_____ Tools	
_____ Books and magazines	
_____ Set of dinnerware	
_____ Lamps	

Combining Like Terms: Graphic Organizer Transparency

Like Terms

x and $-3x$

Combine them: _____

$\frac{1}{2}x^3$ and $5x^3$

Combine them: _____

$7x^2y$ and $-4x^2y$

Combine them: _____

↓ Your Like Terms ↓

Combine them: _____

Combine them: _____

Unlike Terms

$7x$ and $-4y$

Cannot be combined!

x^2 and $5x^3$

Cannot be combined!

$9x^2y$ and $3xy^2$

Cannot be combined!

↓ Your Unlike Terms ↓

Cannot be combined!

Cannot be combined!

Definition of "like terms":

Combining Like Terms: Student Worksheet

Name: _____ Date: _____ Hr: _____

Directions:
For each pair of terms below, (circle) whether the terms are like or unlike and explain why.

1. 17xyz   2xy   Like terms   or   unlike terms

Why? _____

2. $\frac{1}{2}$x   5x   Like terms   or   unlike terms

Why? _____

3. 23b   23c   Like terms   or   unlike terms

Why? _____

4. x x^3 Like terms   or   unlike terms

Why? _____

5. $7x^2y$ $-5x^2y$ Like terms   or   unlike terms

Why? _____

For 6–12, simplify the expressions by combining like terms when possible. If there are no like terms in the expression, write "cannot be combined" on the line.

6. 5v + 7v _____

7. 11w − 6w _____

8. $12y^2$ − 12y _____

9. 7h + $15h^2$ + 3h _____

10. 15b − 5b − 7 _____

11. x + 8y + 9 + 5x − 4y _____

12. 9y + 13 + y^2 − 5y _____

Greatest Common Factor, Two Methods: Teacher Page

Activity 22		
P	**A**	**G**

Content: Comparison of two methods of finding the greatest common factor (GCF)

Standard(s):

About This Activity . . .

This activity is an "old-school" board race where students practice the double-divide method (see Student Handout) to find the GCF of pairs of numbers. Students need to have a solid understanding of common factors and the double-divide method prior to the race to reduce frustration and embarrassment. That said, the race should be used as a follow-up to student worksheets or assignments from the book. Although only five or six students can be at the board at the same time, all students should be doing the work at their seats. The number pairs and their GCFs **(in bold)** are shown below, or you can develop your own list.

---

36 and 40 **GCF: 4**	18 and 24 **GCF: 6**	78 and 104 **GCF: 26**	66 and 72 **GCF: 6**
24 and 54 **GCF: 6**	28 and 40 **GCF: 4**	64 and 80 **GCF: 16**	96 and 120 **GCF: 24**
48 and 72 **GCF: 24**	60 and 72 **GCF: 12**	66 and 110 **GCF: 22**	64 and 84 **GCF: 4**
60 and 48 **GCF: 12**	88 and 72 **GCF: 8**	84 and 112 **GCF: 28**	90 and 150 **GCF: 30**
90 and 60 **GCF: 30**	39 and 52 **GCF: 13**	24 and 84 **GCF: 12**	64 and 112 **GCF: 16**

Bonus: Use the double-divide method to find the GCF of these trios of numbers! The method works the same way with three numbers as with two; you just have an extra number to divide.

36, 72, 84 **GCF: 12**	66, 110, 132 **GCF: 22**	54, 84, 96 **GCF: 6**	54, 126, 90 **GCF: 18**

Name: _____ Date: _____ Hr: _____

Definition: Greatest common factor (GCF)

The greatest common factor is the largest integer that will divide evenly into two or more numbers. The <u>GCF of 4 and 8</u> is 4. The <u>GCF of 12 and 18</u> is 6.

When you are trying to find the GCF of two numbers, one method is to list all of the factors of both numbers and then select the largest factor they have in common. A second method is the double divide. The two methods are compared below.

Method 1: List of Factors

Generating a list of factors for a pair of numbers can be time consuming, especially if the numbers are large.

24: 1, 2, 3, 4, 6, 8, 12, 24

36: 1, 2, 3, 4, 6, 9, 12, 18, 36

Method 2: Double Divide

2 ➔	24	36
2 ➔	12	18
3 ➔	6	9
	2	3

Divide both numbers by the same factors until they have no more common factors. The GCF is the product of the numbers in the left column: $2 \times 2 \times 3$, or 12.

Time to Practice: Find the GCF of 36 and 48 below using the two methods. Then be prepared to explain which method you prefer and why.

Method 1: List of Factors   **Method 2: Double Divide**

Gridlock: Fractions, Decimals, and Percentages: Teacher Page

Content: Pre-algebra: equivalent fractions, decimals, and percentages. Algebra: like terms. Geometry: figures and their names.

Standard(s):

Quick view: In these partner games, students assemble puzzle pieces into a rectangle by matching equivalent terms, figures, and numbers.

The set-up: Run one copy of the game sheet for each pair of students in your classroom. Note: If you run the game sheets on cardstock, one set will hold up for all of your classes. On the game sheet, the grid is not assembled in the correct order, so before you can begin the game, the grid must be cut apart. You can either do this prior to class or have students cut the grids themselves at the beginning of class. Before the game begins, have partners move their desks so they are sitting side-by-side, and explain the game to the class.

The play: Give each pair of students one cut-apart grid. It is their task to reassemble it, matching the items that go together. When the students have completed the grid, they should write the large bold letters from the grid onto a sheet of paper. No letter will be upside down or sideways if the puzzle is completed correctly. If the letter configuration matches the row-by-row solutions at right, they have matched the items correctly. If not, they need to continue working. The winner is the team who correctly completes the puzzle first.

Activity 23
Solutions
Row 1: F G B
Row 2: I C K
Row 3: A L H
Row 4: J E D

Activity 24
Solutions
Row 1: B K C
Row 2: D H A
Row 3: J I E
Row 4: L F G

Activity 25
Solutions
Row 1: R E P L N
Row 2: Q J F B O
Row 3: K M H I C
Row 4: G D S T A

GAME

Gridlock: Fractions, Decimals, and Percentages

Activity 23		
P	A	G

.04 75% **E** $\frac{4}{20}$ $\frac{4}{3}$	25% 15% **H** $\frac{1}{72}$ $\frac{1}{3}$	7.2% $\frac{3}{27}$ **K** .035 $\frac{1}{4}$
$\frac{2}{6}$ $\frac{1}{5}$ **D** .1 1.8	$\frac{2}{7}$ .5 **B** $\frac{4}{5}$ .072	90% 10% **G** $\frac{1}{2}$ $\frac{14}{8}$
$\frac{3}{18}$ $\frac{8}{9}$ **A** $\frac{2}{3}$ .003	18% 5% **F** $\frac{1}{10}$ .72	72% .6 **I** .37 $\frac{1}{6}$
$\frac{3}{1000}$ $\frac{3}{21}$ **J** $\frac{3}{4}$ .03	35% $-$ .6 **L** $\frac{3}{20}$ 4%	$1\frac{3}{4}$ $\frac{37}{100}$ **C** $\frac{1}{9}$ .350

From *Making Math Accessible for the At-Risk Student: Grades 7–12* by Linda Ptacek. Santa Barbara, CA: Libraries Unlimited. Copyright © 2011.

GAME

Gridlock: Like Terms

$-\dfrac{1}{2}abc$	$12f^3$	ab
$9u^2$ **E** $6x$	$2wxy$ **H** $-3b^2c^2$	$7mn$ **K** $7rs^2$
$3h^2$	fx	$17f^3$
$-4x^2$	gf^2	$\dfrac{1}{2}h^2$
$4v^2$ **D** $3wxy$	$14w$ **B** $3mn$	$2v^4$ **G** $5x^3$
$2k$	$2x^2$	$17r^2s$
$-2de$	$4xyz$	$5fx$
$4b^2c^2$ **A** km	$-6w$ **F** $11v^4$	$7a^2b$ **I** u^2
$4abc$	ab^2	$9xyz$
$-6k$	c	xy^2
$3wx$ **J** $2a^2b$	$17mh$ **L** $14w$	$\dfrac{1}{2}rs^2$ **C** $3h$
$9c$	$3d^2e$	$14de$

GAME

Gridlock: Geometry Terms

hexagon) **A** vertical angles radius perimeter	point **B** 	supplementary ∠s hypotenuse **C** decagon 	circumference **D**
$a^2 + b^2 = c^2$ pyramid **E**	semicircle **F** cube	cone **G** area central angle	trapezoid **H** pentagon
ray ellipse **I**	quadrilateral **J** diagonal	volume vertex **K** collinear points	isosceles △ protractor **L** perpendicular lines
right angle **M** acute angle	bisect **N** vertical angl 	equilateral △ chord **O** diagonal	complementary ∠s degree **P** line
sphere tangent **Q** parallel lines A	prism cylinder **R** Pythagorean Theorem	diameter **S** obtuse △ heptagon	segment **T** arc octagon

Linear Equations: Teacher Pages

Content: Counting slope, calculating slope, slope-intercept form, graphing in slope-intercept form, horizontal and vertical lines, parallel and perpendicular lines

Standard(s):

About These Activities . . .

Activities 26–31 review different elements of linear equations. The focus of each activity is outlined below along with a brief description. Each of the handouts is intended to be a teacher-facilitated review, not a homework assignment. Each could also be used to introduce the topics initially, but additional practice problems would be needed at each step. Solutions for all worksheets follow Activity 31.

Activity 26: Counting the Slope of a Line

Students are often confused by this step because "rise over run" addresses the y-values first, while plotting points identifies the x-value first. Emphasize the hotel analogy on the student handout to help clarify the "rise over run" order.

Activity 27: Calculating Slope Given Two Points

This page introduces positive, negative, zero, and undefined slopes as well as the slope formula. To use the slope formula, have students stack the ordered pairs and circle the y-values since they start with those, then subtract. This eliminates the errors made going from one ordered pair to the other. Remind the students that this method is much quicker than drawing a graph and plotting points to count the slope. After instruction, give the students a dozen pairs of points on which to practice calculating slope. Make sure you have three of each type that was introduced: positive, negative, zero, and undefined.

Activity 28: What Is Slope-Intercept Form?

This activity is designed to reinforce the position of the slope and y-intercept in linear equations and also to remind students to always make a fraction out of the slope to get both a rise and a run.

Activity 29: Graphing in Slope-Intercept Form

In this activity, students review graphing using the slope-intercept form. Remind them to **b**egin with the **b** (y-intercept) and then **m**ove on to the **m** (slope) when they graph these equations. Repeat the same wording as you model each problem to help with retention.

Activity 30: Horizontal and Vertical Lines

Read the HOY-VUX limericks aloud to the class and discuss the benefits of using memory aids like mnemonics or poems to solidify new information. "In 1492, Columbus sailed the ocean blue." Proceed to the student handout and work through the problems as a group. When all of the graphs are completed, ask the students to identify each one as HOY or VUX.

Activity 31: Parallel and Perpendicular Lines

Students quickly grasp that parallel lines have the same slope, but they have more difficulty with perpendicular lines. To illustrate "same vs. inverse reciprocal," count the slopes of the lines in the examples at the top of the student handout. Since *inverse reciprocals* is a big mouthful, a quick way to remember perpendicular slopes is FLIP IT-SWITCH IT. Flip the fraction; switch the sign. Orally, give students a dozen slopes to practice FLIP IT-SWITCH IT on. Then do a dozen more slopes, this time randomly asking for the slope parallel or perpendicular to the one given. Finally, when you are sure the students understand the concept, move on to the worksheet.

REVIEW

Linear Equations 1: Counting the Slope of a Line

Name: _____ Date: _____ Hr: _____

Imagine your family is staying in a big hotel with another family, but you are on different floors. If you want to get to your friends' room, you have to go up or down the elevator first, <u>then</u> go to their room. You do the same thing when you count the slope of a line.

To count the slope of a line, follow these four steps:

1. Locate any two points on the line. You will start counting from the farthest LEFT point of the two.

2. Count the number of spaces up/down (called the "rise") needed to get to the level of the other point. Remember, take the elevator up (positive) or down (negative).

3. Now count the number of spaces right (called the "run") to arrive at the second point. Compare this to "running" down the hall to get to the right room.

4. Now make a fraction out of the rise number over the run number and reduce it: **rise** / **run**

In the graphs below, count the slope of each line and write it on the correct blank.

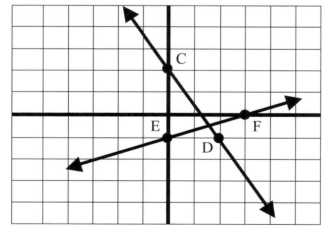
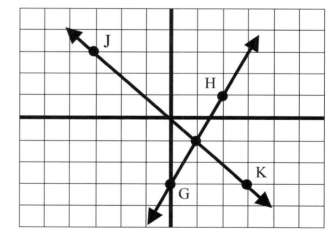

Line CD _____   Line EF _____   Line GH _____   Line JK _____

Linear Equations 1: Counting the Slope of a Line

Name: _____ Date: _____ Hr: _____

1. Plot (3, 4) and (−2, 1) and count the slope of that line.

2. Plot (−4, 4) and (1, −4) and count the slope of that line.

3. Plot (−2, −3) and (4, 0) and count the slope of that line.

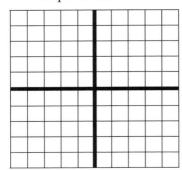 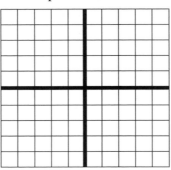 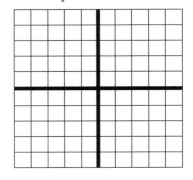

4. Draw a line through (−4, −2) with a slope of $\frac{3}{4}$.

5. Draw a line through (0, 0) with a slope of 4.

6. Draw a line through (−2, 4) with a slope of $-\frac{7}{4}$.

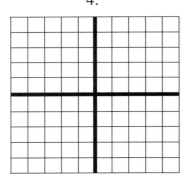 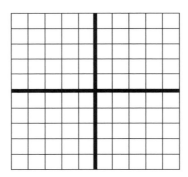 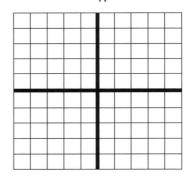

7. Draw a line with a slope of $\frac{2}{5}$.

8. Draw a line with a slope of −3.

9. Draw a line with a slope of 2.

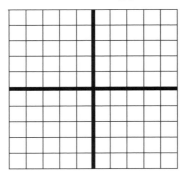 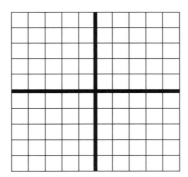 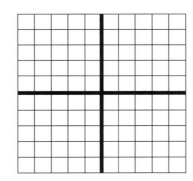

REVIEW

Linear Equations 2: Calculating Slope Given Two Points

	Activity 27	
P	A	G

Name: _____ Date: _____ Hr: _____

Linear equations can have one of four types of slope: positive, negative, zero, or undefined.

Positive	Negative	Zero	Undefined
$\frac{5}{7}$	$-\frac{3}{2}$	$\frac{0}{7}$	$\frac{4}{0}$
"uphill"	"downhill"	"horizontal"	"vertical"

If you know any two points on a line, you can calculate that line's slope or steepness with a formula instead of plotting the points and counting the slope. The letter **m** in the formula below stands for **slope**. The top number in the slope's fraction represents the "rise" and the bottom number is the "run." If your slope is a whole number like 5, the bottom number (or run) is always 1.

The formula:	The example:	The process:	The answer:
$m = \dfrac{y_2 - y_1}{x_2 - x_1}$	Calculate the slope of a line through the points $(2, 5)$ and $(-1, 4)$ $\downarrow \downarrow \quad \downarrow \downarrow$ $(x_1, y_1) \quad (x_2, y_2)$	Stack the ordered pairs and subtract. Start with the y-values. $(-1, 4)$ $-(2, 5)$	$\dfrac{4-5}{-1-2} = \dfrac{-1}{-3}$ Reduce or simplify the fraction if possible. $\dfrac{1}{3}$

Practice Problems: Calculate the slope of the line through each pair of points below. Remember to stack your ordered pairs and circle the y-values first. Show all steps.

1. (3, 9) and (1, 6)   2. (0, 4) and (3, –2)   3. (1, 6) and (3, 4)

Linear Equations 3: What Is Slope-Intercept Form?

	Activity 28
P	**A**	**G**

Name: _____ Date: _____ Hr: _____

The equation y = **m**x + **b** is called the slope-intercept form of an equation. When linear equations are written in this form, graphing them is simple. The number in front of x (its coefficient) is the slope of the line. The slope measures the line's steepness. The number without a variable (the constant) is the y-intercept of the line. The y-intercept tells where the line crosses the y-axis. If there is no y-intercept in the equation, the line crosses the y-axis at (0,0).

$$y = \mathbf{m}x + \mathbf{b}$$
$$\downarrow \qquad \downarrow$$
slope   y-intercept

$$y = \mathbf{7}x \boxed{-\ \mathbf{5}}$$
$$\downarrow \qquad \downarrow$$
slope   y-intercept

Directions: Identify the slope, rise, run, and y-intercept of each line below. Remember, the "rise" is the top number of the slope. The "run" is the bottom number (or 1 if the slope is a whole number). If the slope is negative, keep the negative sign with the "rise" number.

	Equation	Slope (m)	Rise	Run	Y-Intercept (b)
1.	$y = 5x - 8$	5	5	1	−8
2.	$y = x + 6$				
3.	$y = \frac{2}{3}x$				
4.	$y = \frac{1}{6}x - 3$				
5.	$y = 3x - 12$				
6.	$y = -\frac{3}{8}x - 9$				
7.	$y = 4x + 3$				
8.	$y = x - 5$				
9.	$y = -2x - 1$				
10.	$y = -\frac{5}{3}x$				

Linear Equations 4: Graphing Equations in Slope-Intercept Form

Activity 29		
P	A	G

Name: _____ Date: _____ Hr: _____

In slope-intercept form, you have all the information you need to graph a line:

$$y = \mathbf{m}x + \mathbf{b}$$
$$\downarrow \qquad \downarrow$$
slope   y-intercept

$$y = \mathbf{7}x \;\boxed{-\,5}$$
$$\downarrow \qquad \downarrow$$
slope   y-intercept

Here is a hint to help you remember how to graph: <u>B</u>egin with the "**b**," then <u>m</u>ove on to the "**m**." Here are three examples to show you how it's done.

Example 1

$$y = \frac{2}{3}x - 4$$

The slope of the line is $\frac{2}{3}$ and the y-intercept is –4.

First plot the y-intercept. Go down the y-axis to –4 and make a point.

Next, use your slope number to rise 2 and run 3. <u>Always run to the right.</u> Put another point at that location.

Finally, connect the points with a line.

Example 2

$$y = -x + 3$$

When there is no number in front of the x use "1." So, the slope of this line is –1 (or $-\frac{1}{1}$). The y-intercept is 3.

Plot the y-intercept. Go up the y-axis to 3 and make a point.

Next, use your slope number to go down –1 and run 1. <u>Always run to the right.</u> Put another point at that location.

Finally, connect the points with a line.

Example 3

$$y = -\frac{3}{4}x$$

The slope of the line is $-\frac{3}{4}$ and since there is no y-intercept shown, it is 0.

Plot the y-intercept. Make a point at the origin (0, 0).

Next, use your slope number to go down –3 and run 4. <u>Always run to the right.</u> Put another point at that location.

Finally, connect the points with a line.

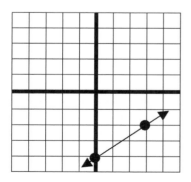
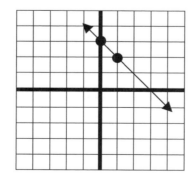
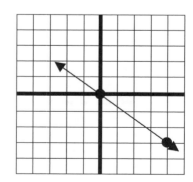

Linear Equations 4: Graphing Equations in Slope-Intercept Form

	Activity 29	
P	**A**	**G**

Name: _____ Date:_____ Hr:_____

Directions: Graph each of the equations below using its slope and the y-intercept. Circle the y-intercept in each equation before you start, to show that locating it will be your first step.

1. $y = 2x - 4$

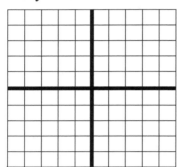

2. $y = -3x + 2$

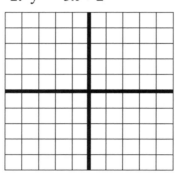

3. $y = x + 2$

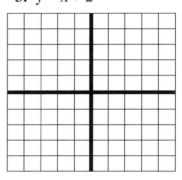

4. $y = -\dfrac{3}{2}x$

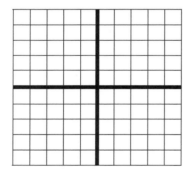

5. $y = -\dfrac{1}{5}x - 1$

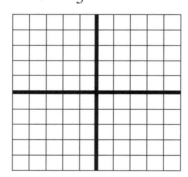

6. $y = \dfrac{4}{3}x - 4$

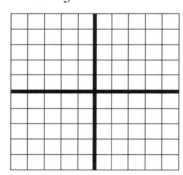

7. $y = -\dfrac{4}{3}x + 4$

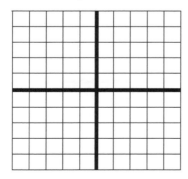

8. $y = -\dfrac{1}{4}x - 3$

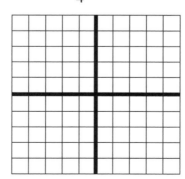

9. $y = -2x - 2$

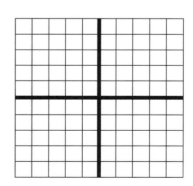

From *Making Math Accessible for the At-Risk Student: Grades 7–12* by Linda Ptacek. Santa Barbara, CA: Libraries Unlimited. Copyright © 2011.

Linear Equations 5: Horizontal and Vertical Lines

	Activity 30	
P	A	G

Name: _____ Date: _____ Hr: _____

Directions: Graph each of the lines and equations using what you know about HOY and VUX.

1. Slope of 0, through (2, 3)

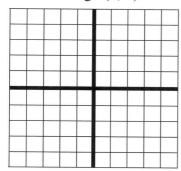

2. Slope of 0, through (−4, −2)

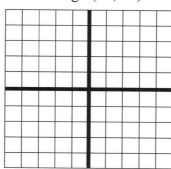

3. Undefined slope, through (2, 3)

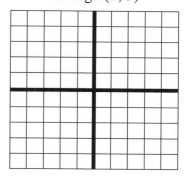

4. Undefined slope, through (−4, −2)

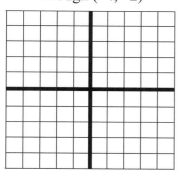

5. Graph x = 2

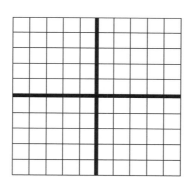

6. Graph y = 4

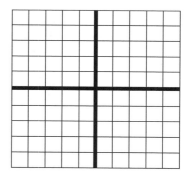

7. Graph y = −1

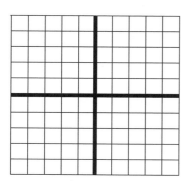

8. Graph x = −3

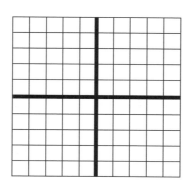

9. Write the equation of this line.

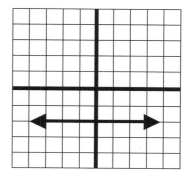

Linear Equations 5: Horizontal and Vertical Lines

Name: _____ Date: _____ Hr: _____

HOY and VUX, A Limerick

Two knights of the Round Table name

Enjoyed playing a linear game.

King Arthur said, "Fine,

You can graph all our lines.

Let that be your own claim to fame!"

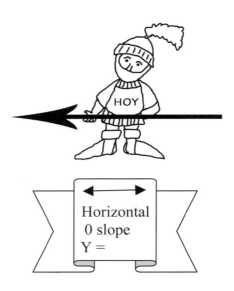

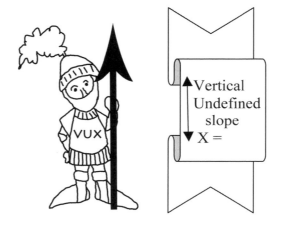

HOY graphed only one type of line.

"Horizontal and flat; those are mine!

I love zero slope

Just like a tightrope

And y = a number is fine."

His brother, VUX, did not agree.

"Vertical is the best line for me.

It's slope's undefined,

But I don't even mind.

There's an x = number guarantee."

Linear Equations 6: Parallel and Perpendicular Lines

Name: _____ Date: _____ Hr: _____

Example 1: Parallel lines
never intersect (cross)

Example 2: Perpendicular lines
intersect at a 90° angle

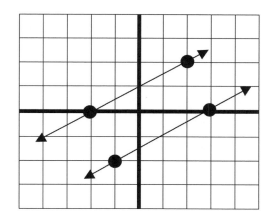

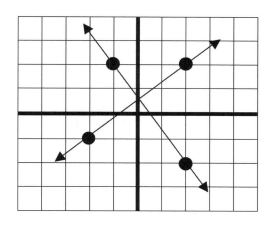

Parallel, Perpendicular, or Neither?

If equations are written in slope-intercept form, it is easy to tell if they are parallel, perpendicular, or neither by looking at their slopes.

Parallel Lines	Perpendicular Lines	Neither
$y = 7x + 6$ $y = 7x - 11$	$y = 2x + 8$ $y = -\frac{1}{2}x - 5$	$y = -3x - 9$ $y = -\frac{1}{3}x + 12$
Since parallel lines never intersect, they <u>must</u> have the same slope.	These lines are perpendicular and their slopes are opposite reciprocals. (Flip the slope upside down and switch the sign.) **FLIP IT—SWITCH IT**	These equations are neither parallel nor perpendicular. Their slopes are reciprocals, but their signs are the same.

Linear Equations 6: Parallel and Perpendicular Lines

Name: _____ Date: _____ Hr: _____

Directions: Use your handout on parallel and perpendicular lines to answer the following questions. Circle the correct response.

---

1. Which equation below is <u>parallel</u> to the line $y = 3x + 22$?

    A. $y = -3x - 22$
    B. $y = 3x + 8$
    C. $y = \frac{1}{3} x - 14$

2. Which equation below is <u>perpendicular</u> to the line $y = -\frac{2}{7} x - 3$?

    A. $y = -\frac{2}{7} x + 14$

    B. $y = \frac{7}{2} x + 3$

    C. $y = 7x + 2$

---

3. The lines $y = \frac{1}{4} x - 6$ and $y = -4x - 5$ are _____.

    A. perpendicular
    B. parallel
    C. neither parallel nor perpendicular

4. The lines $y = 5x + 7$ and $y = -5x - 7$ are _____.

    A. parallel
    B. perpendicular
    C. neither parallel nor perpendicular

---

5. Look at these equations:

$y = -\frac{1}{4} x + 9$ and $y = -\frac{1}{4} x - 9$

They form <u>parallel</u> lines because

    A. they are in slope-intercept form.
    B. their slopes are the same.
    C. the y-intercepts are different.

6. The equation of a line is $x = 5$. What is the equation of a line <u>perpendicular</u> to this line?

    A. $y = -7$

    B. $x = -\frac{1}{5}$

    C. undefined

---

7. If a line like $x = -2$ has an undefined slope, what is the slope of a line parallel to it?

    A. 0
    B. 1
    C. undefined

8. Explain why these two lines are neither parallel nor perpendicular.

$y = \frac{1}{2} x + 6$ and $y = 2x - 6$

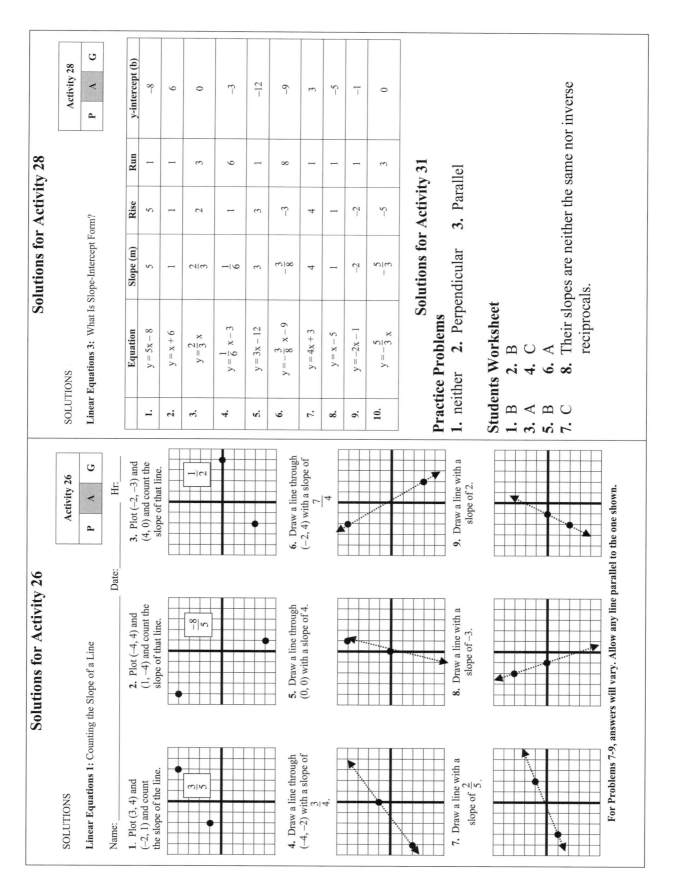

Solutions for Activity 26

SOLUTIONS

Linear Equations 1: Counting the Slope of a Line

| Activity 26 |
| P | A | G |

Name: _____ Date: _____ Hr: _____

1. Plot (3, 4) and (−2, 1) and count the slope of the line. $\frac{3}{5}$

2. Plot (−4, 4) and (1, −4) and count the slope of that line. $\frac{-8}{5}$

3. Plot (−2, −3) and (4, 0) and count the slope of that line. $\frac{1}{2}$

4. Draw a line through (−4, −2) with a slope of $\frac{3}{4}$.

5. Draw a line through (0, 0) with a slope of 4.

6. Draw a line through (−2, 4) with a slope of $\frac{7}{4}$

7. Draw a line with a slope of $\frac{2}{5}$.

8. Draw a line with a slope of −3.

9. Draw a line with a slope of 2.

For Problems 7–9, answers will vary. Allow any line parallel to the one shown.

Solutions for Activity 28

SOLUTIONS

Linear Equations 3: What Is Slope-Intercept Form?

| Activity 28 |
| P | A | G |

	Equation	Slope (m)	Rise	Run	y-intercept (b)
1.	$y = 5x - 8$	5	5	1	−8
2.	$y = x + 6$	1	1	1	6
3.	$y = \frac{2}{3}x$	$\frac{2}{3}$	2	3	0
4.	$y = \frac{1}{6}x - 3$	$\frac{1}{6}$	1	6	−3
5.	$y = 3x - 12$	3	3	1	−12
6.	$y = -\frac{3}{8}x - 9$	$-\frac{3}{8}$	−3	8	−9
7.	$y = 4x + 3$	4	4	1	3
8.	$y = x - 5$	1	1	1	−5
9.	$y = -2x - 1$	−2	−2	1	−1
10.	$y = -\frac{5}{3}x$	$-\frac{5}{3}$	−5	3	0

Solutions for Activity 31

Practice Problems

1. neither **2.** Perpendicular **3.** Parallel

Students Worksheet

1. B   **2.** B
3. A   **4.** C
5. B   **6.** A
7. C   **8.** Their slopes are neither the same nor inverse reciprocals.

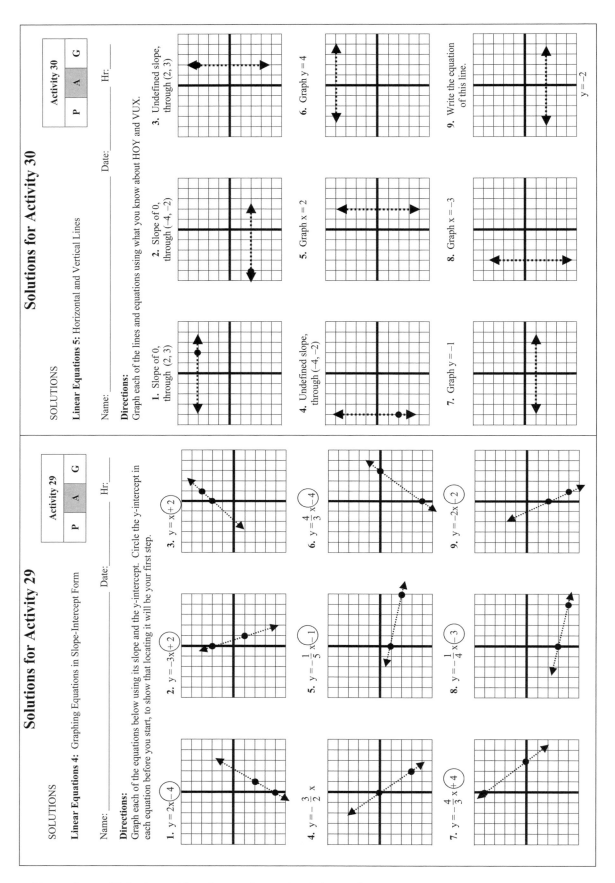

Solutions for Activity 30

SOLUTIONS

Linear Equations 5: Horizontal and Vertical Lines

Name: _____ Date: _____ Hr: _____

Directions:
Graph each of the lines and equations using what you know about HOY and VUX.

1. Slope of 0, through (2, 3)

2. Slope of 0, through (−4, −2)

3. Undefined slope, through (2, 3)

4. Undefined slope, through (−4, −2)

5. Graph x = 2

6. Graph y = 4

7. Graph y = −1

8. Graph x = −3

9. Write the equation of this line.

y = −2

Solutions for Activity 29

SOLUTIONS

Linear Equations 4: Graphing Equations in Slope-Intercept Form

Name: _____ Date: _____ Hr: _____

Directions:
Graph each of the equations below using its slope and the y-intercept. Circle the y-intercept in each equation before you start, to show that locating it will be your first step.

1. $y = 2x \circ{-4}$

2. $y = -3x \circ{+2}$

3. $y = x \circ{+2}$

4. $y = -\frac{3}{2}x$

5. $y = -\frac{1}{5}x \circ{-1}$

6. $y = \frac{4}{3}x \circ{-4}$

7. $y = -\frac{4}{3}x \circ{+4}$

8. $y = -\frac{1}{4}x \circ{-3}$

9. $y = -2x \circ{-2}$

Number Tag: A Real Numbers Song

Name: _____   Date: _____   Hr: _____

To be sung to the tune of "JINGLE BELLS"

1,2,3,... 1,2,3,... **NATURALS** are we.
Add a zero to our set
And we're **WHOLE** as can be.
1,2,3,... 1,2,3,... **NATURALS** are we.
Add a zero to our set
And we're **WHOLE** as can be.

Every whole number
Has an opposite, you see.
1 and then there's –1,
The **INTEGERS** are we.

1,2,3,... 1,2,3,... **NATURALS** are we.
Add a zero to our set
And we're **WHOLE** as can be.
1,2,3,... 1,2,3,... **NATURALS** are we.
Add a zero to our set
And we're **WHOLE** as can be.

There needs to be a place
For all fractions to go.
Take the decimals along
And call them **RATIONAL**.

1,2,3,... 1,2,3,... **NATURALS** are we.
Add a zero to our set
And we're **WHOLE** as can be.
1,2,3,... 1,2,3,... **NATURALS** are we.
Add a zero to our set
And we're **WHOLE** as can be.

Some decimals don't end;
They never do repeat.
IRRATIONAL's the only term
For numbers oh so sweet!

1,2,3,... 1,2,3,... **NATURALS** are we.
Add a zero to our set
And we're **WHOLE** as can be.
1,2,3,... 1,2,3,... **NATURALS** are we.
Add a zero to our set
And we're **WHOLE** as can be.

These number sets you've heard
All fit into one bag.
We call them **REAL NUMBERS** and
You've just played Number Tag!

LESSON

Mean, Median, Mode, and Range: Teacher Page

Content: Measures of central tendency

Standard(s):

Activity 33		
P	**A**	**G**

About This Activity . . .

For this activity, each student needs a copy of the "Mean, Median, Mode, and Range" handout, a blank sheet of notebook paper, and the lyrics to the mean, median, mode song (see chapter 4). Introduce mean, median, mode, and range with the song and the handout. Discuss each term thoroughly, doing as many examples as necessary. For the next part of the activity, if necessary, move students around to make the number of students in each row similar or equal. The data you will be analyzing for this activity will be generated by the students using their responses to the questions below. Ask each row a question and give them one minute to write down their responses. The <u>number</u> of answers each student writes down will become the data for their row. Write the data on the board, row by row. On the sheet of notebook paper, students will then find the mean, median, mode, and range for their row's numbers. For additional practice, rotate the rows through all sets of data.

> **Row 1:** Name as many vegetables as you can in one minute.
>
> **Row 2:** Name as many singers as you can in one minute.
>
> **Row 3:** Name as many TV programs as you can in one minute.
>
> **Row 4:** Name as many desserts as you can in one minute.
>
> **Row 5:** Name as many pieces of furniture as you can in one minute.
>
> **Row 6:** Name as many cars as you can in one minute.

Mean, Median, Mode, and Range: Student Handout

Name: _____ Date: _____ Hr: _____

Term	Description	How to Figure
Mean	The mean is sometimes called the "average" of a set of numbers. To find the mean, add the numbers and divide the total by how many numbers you have.	$$\dfrac{7+2+8+4+3+6}{6}$$
Median	Arrange the numbers from smallest to largest. The median is now the middle number in the group. If there is no "middle number," find the mean of the middle <u>two</u>.	**Ex. 1:** 2 3 **8** 9 10 **Ex. 2:** 2 3 **8 10** 11 17 What is the mean of 8 and 10? **9** (Add them and divide by 2.)
Mode	Mode is the number that appears most often in the set of data. There can be no mode, one mode, or more than one mode.	**Ex. 1:** This group has no mode. 12 8 88 91 13 **Ex. 2:** This group has one mode. **8 8** 18 19 97 **Ex. 3:** This group has two modes. **8 8** 88 **90 90** 97
Range	Range is the difference between the largest and smallest numbers in a set. Just subtract them.	**8** 9 10 15 **19** $19 - 8 = 11$

From *Making Math Accessible for the At-Risk Student: Grades 7–12* by Linda Ptacek. Santa Barbara, CA: Libraries Unlimited. Copyright © 2011.

LESSON

Multiplying Binomials, Check-Double-Check: Teacher Page

Content: Multiplying a pair of binomials using two different methods

Standard(s):

About This Activity . . .

This check-double-check activity, designed for partners, practices two different methods for multiplying pairs of binomials: the **FOIL** method and the **BOXES** method. Teach students both methods, doing several practice problems.

FOIL

$(4x + 5)(2x - 3)$
$8x^2 - 12x + 10x - 15$
$8x^2 - 2x - 15$

For students who cannot keep track of which terms they have FOILed, the BOXES method at right seems to be a helpful organizer.

BOXES

$(4x + 5)(2x - 3)$

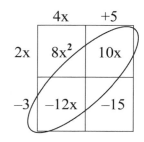

$8x^2 - 12x + 10x - 15$
$8x^2 - 2x - 15$

After the instruction, pair up students and assign each partner a letter (X or Y). "X" students do problems 1–6 with the FOIL method and problems 7–12 with the BOXES method. Reverse the methods for the "Y" students. When they have finished the problems, they should compare answers and correct problems if necessary. Afterward, have a class discussion comparing and contrasting the methods.

Solutions

1. $c^2 - 3c - 18$

2. $y^2 - 11y + 24$

3. $x^2 - 1$

4. $4x^2 + 8x - 5$

5. $4x^2 - 7x - 2$

6. $9b^2 - 3b - 20$

7. $w^2 + 11w + 24$

8. $v^2 - 11v + 30$

9. $n^2 - 14n + 49$

10. $2k^2 - 10k - 28$

11. $9x^2 - 4$

12. $5c^2 - 32c - 21$

LESSON

Multiplying Binomials, Check-Double-Check

Name: _____ Date: _____ Hr: _____

Set 1: Teacher will assign the method to use on this set.

1. $(c + 3)(c - 6)$	**2.** $(y - 8)(y - 3)$	**3.** $(x + 1)(x - 1)$
4. $(2x - 1)(2x + 5)$	**5.** $(4x + 1)(x - 2)$	**6.** $(3b + 4)(3b - 5)$

Set 2: Teacher will assign the method to use on this set.

7. $(w + 8)(w + 3)$	**8.** $(v - 6)(v - 5)$	**9.** $(n - 7)(n - 7)$
10. $(2k + 4)(k - 7)$	**11.** $(3x + 2)(3x - 2)$	**12.** $(5c + 3)(c - 7)$

LESSON

Order of Operations: Teacher Page

Content: Order of operations

Standard(s):

About This Activity . . .

This activity reviews the mnemonic device PEMDAS (Please Excuse My Dear Aunt Sally) as a tool to help students remember the order of operations. In the first worksheet, students are instructed to identify only the first step of the process for a set of problems. After they feel comfortable getting started, the second worksheet asks them to work the entire problem. Because of the number of errors at-risk students seem to make in copying problems onto their own paper, they have been given ample room to do the problems on the worksheet.

Solutions for Order of Operations, What Is Your First Step?

1. 8×3 **2.** 2^2 **3.** $(7-1)$ **4.** 2^2 **5.** 8×2 **6.** $(5+4)$ **7.** 2^2 **8.** $(6-4)$

9. (4×9) **10.** 3×5 **11.** 3^2 **12.** $(6+3)$ **13.** $(4 \div 2)$ **14.** $30 \div 10$ **15.** $(12 \div 4)$

Solutions for Order of Operations Worksheet 2

1. 13   **2.** 12   **3.** 24   **4.** 13   **5.** 8   **6.** 40   **7.** 19   **8.** 105

9. 8   **10.** 17   **11.** 12   **12.** 9   **13.** 48   **14.** 52   **15.** 4   **16.** 1

17. 18   **18.** 24

Solutions for Order of Operations Worksheet 3

1. D   **2.** C   **3.** A   **4.** E   **5.** B   **6.** H   **7.** F   **8.** I   **9.** J   **10.** G

LESSON

Order of Operations: Student Worksheet 1

Name: _____ Date: _____ Hr: _____

When you have to do math problems with several operations ($+ \; - \; \times \; \div$), there is a "right" order and a "wrong" order. To help remember the correct order of operations, people use the phrase, "Please excuse my dear Aunt Sally." Each letter represents a different step of the process. Not every problem has all six steps, but you still have to check for each one.

Parentheses….	Do any work inside of **Parentheses**.	$7 + 2 \times 3^2 - \textbf{(8 − 2)} \div 3$
Exponents……	Calculate each **Exponent**.	$7 + 2 \times \textbf{3}^\textbf{2} - 6 \div 3$
{ **M**ultiplication….	Do all **Multiplication** and **Division** in	$7 + \textbf{2 x 9} - \textbf{6} \div \textbf{3}$
Division	order from left to right.	
{ **A**ddition………	Do all **Addition** and **Subtraction** in	$\textbf{7 + 18 − 2}$
Subtraction	order from left to right.	23

Ex. 1: $3 \times 4^2 \div (8 - 2)$ Ex. 2: $4^2 + (8 \div 2) - 3$
          $3 \times 4^2 \div 6$ $4^2 + 4 \; - 3$
          $3 \times 16 \div 6$ $16 + 4 \; - 3$
              $48 \div 6$ $20 \; - 3$
                  8   17

Directions: For each of the problems below, decide which of the two choices following it shows the correct first step. <u>Do not calculate the answer!</u>

		Circle the correct first step below.
1.	$7 + 8 \times 3 \div 6 - 6$	$7 + 8$ or 8×3
2.	$3 + 9 \times 4 \div 12 - 2^2$	2^2 or 9×4
3.	$20 - 18 \div (7 - 1) \times 3$	$(7 - 1)$ or $20 - 18$

4.	$5 \times 2^2 + 9$	5×2	or	2^2
5.	$3 + 8 \times 2 \div 8$	$3 + 8$	or	8×2
6.	$20 - (5 + 4) \div (12 - 3)$	$20 - 5$	or	$(5 + 4)$
7.	$8 \div 2^2 + 22 \div 11$	2^2	or	$22 \div 11$
8.	$5 + 4^2 \div (6 - 4)$	$(6 - 4)$	or	4^2
9.	$14 + (4 \times 9) \div 6^2$	(4×9)	or	6^2
10.	$6 + 3 \times 5 - 2$	$6 + 3$	or	3×5
11.	$3 + 18 \div 3^2 - 5$	3^2	or	$3 + 18$
12.	$3^2 - (6 + 3) + 4 \times 2$	3^2	or	$(6 + 3)$
13.	$10 - 3(4 \div 2) + 3^2$	$10 - 3$	or	$(4 \div 2)$
14.	$17 + 30 \div 10 - 8 \times 2$	$17 + 30$	or	$30 \div 10$
15.	$(12 \div 4)^2 + 18 \div 3$	$(12 \div 4)$	or	$18 \div 3$

Order of Operations: Student Worksheet 2

	Activity 35
	P | **A** | **G**

Name: _____ Date: _____ Hr: _____

Directions: Perform the correct order of operations to find these answers.

1.	$3 + 5 \times 2$	**2.**	$10 + 10 \div 5$
3.	$3 \times 7 + 15 \div 5$	**4.**	$15 - (8 - 6)$
5.	$2 \times 3 + 5 - 3$	**6.**	$7 + 5(4 + 3) - 14 \div 7$
7.	$4 + 3 \times 2^3 - 3^2$	**8.**	$10^2 - 5 \times 4 + 5^2$

9.	$2 + (3 + 5) - 18 \div 9$	**10.**	$12 + 4 \times 3 - (28 \div 4)$
11.	$20 - 3 (10 - 3 \times 2) + 4$	**12.**	$9 + 2 (7 - 5) - 36 \div 3^2$
13.	$(3 + 2)^2 \times 2 - (4^2 \div 8)$	**14.**	$2 + (4^2 \div 8) \times (3 + 2)^2$
15.	$2 + (3 + 5) \times 2^3 \div 32$	**16.**	$36 \div (3^2 + 6^2 - 9)$
17.	$5^2 - (6 + 3) + 4 \div 2$	**18.**	$5^2 - 6 + 3 + 4 \div 2$

LESSON

Order of Operations: Student Worksheet 3

Name: _____ Date: _____ Hr: _____

Directions: Use what you know about the order of operations to match the expression in the first column with its answer in the second column.

<u>Set 1:</u> Match choices A–E to the first five problems.

1. _____ $6 + 3 \times 5 - 3$ **A.** 14

2. _____ $3 + 8 \times 2 \div 8$ **B.** 6

3. _____ $20 - 18 \div (4 + 5) \times 3$ **C.** 5

4. _____ $5 \times 2^2 + 9$ **D.** 18

5. _____ $4 + (8 \times 9) \div 6^2$ **E.** 29

<u>Set 2:</u> Match choices F–J to these five problems.

6. _____ $20 - (5 \times 3) \div (12 + 3)$ **F.** 8

7. _____ $18 \div 3^2 + 12 \div 2$ **G.** 9

8. _____ $5 + 8^2 \div (6 - 4)$ **H.** 19

9. _____ $7 + 8 \times 3 \div 12 - 6$ **I.** 37

10. _____ $3 + 8 \times 6 \div (12 - 2^2)$ **J.** 3

LESSON

Parallel Lines and Transversals: Teacher Page

Content: Bisect, intersect, parallel lines, transversal

Standard(s):

About This Activity . . .

This activity is designed for the special education student who is working significantly below grade level in a high school geometry class and whose work must be modified. It allows students to focus on a reduced number of concepts verbally, graphically, and in verse. It could be done one-on-one or in a small group setting led by a special education teacher or support personnel. The content is introduced with a limerick, a bit of a surprise in a math class! Four additional limericks have been included after the Student Worksheet for the teacher to use when planning other lessons. As an extension of this lesson, students could identify photos showing parallel lines to demonstrate their mastery of the concepts. For example, given 10 photos, ask the student to sort them into two stacks, those <u>with</u> parallel lines and those <u>without</u> parallel lines.

LESSON

Parallel Lines and Transversals: Student Worksheet

Name: _____ Date: _____ Hr: _____

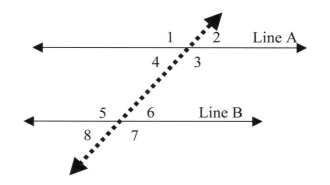

There once were two **parallel lines**
Whose paths never crossed anytime.
A **transversal** ran through
Bisecting their view,
And creating eight angles so fine.

Vocabulary	What It Looks Like	Your Turn
Bisect: To cut exactly in half; to cut into two equal parts.	These two line segments bisect each other.	Bisect this line.
Intersect: To cross or meet.	These pairs of lines intersect.	Draw two lines that intersect.
Parallel Lines: Lines that never cross (intersect). They are always the same distance apart. A shortcut for writing "Line A is parallel to Line B" is A $\|$ B	These lines are parallel.	Draw a pair of parallel lines.
Transversal: A line that crosses two parallel lines is called a transversal.	The transversal is the dotted line.	Draw a transversal across these lines.

Parallel Lines and Transversals: Student Worksheet

Name: _____ Date: _____ Hr: _____

1. Draw a line segment that bisects each of these segments.

2. Which of the following pairs of lines are parallel? Circle the || lines.

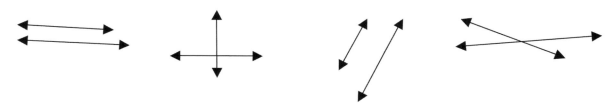

3. Draw a transversal across each pair of parallel lines shown below.

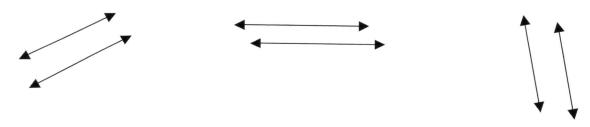

Use the symbol for parallel lines || to state which lines below are parallel.
If they are not parallel, leave the line underneath them blank. One has been done.

Example:	4.	5.	6.

A || B _____ _____ _____

From *Making Math Accessible for the At-Risk Student: Grades 7–12* by Linda Ptacek. Santa Barbara, CA: Libraries Unlimited. Copyright © 2011.

LESSON

Limericks and Lingo: Teacher Page

Content: Four limericks to introduce new math vocabulary

Standard(s):

Line graphs are like people you meet.

Some are **positive**, uplifting, and sweet.

But some bring you down,

Turn a smile to a frown.

They're so **negative** that you want to retreat.

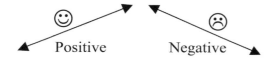

Positive   Negative

Radius and **Diameter** made a bet

To race across a circle they'd met.

Poor Radius stopped short;

He only made it half-court,

But Diameter crossed it, no sweat!

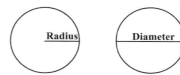

Prime numbers are all **factor**-poor

Just 1 and the number, no more.

Composites are rich

With factors – no hitch!

But to tell them apart is a chore!

Prime: 2, 3, 5, 7, 11, 13, 17, 19, 23, …

Composite: 4, 6, 8, 9, 10, 12, 14, 15, …

The **segment**, the **line**, and the **ray**

Were discussing their math roles one day.

"No **endpoints** have I,"

Said the line with a sigh,

"But my path can lead any which way!"

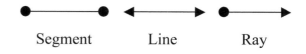

Segment   Line   Ray

LESSON

Parallel Lines, Transversals, and the Angles They Form: Teacher
Page

Content: Parallel lines, transversals, and the angles they form

Standard(s):

About This Activity . . .	**Solutions**
Somehow students always make this concept more difficult than it really is. Start with a quick review of the nine types of angles in Activity 5, and then explain that you will be introducing the class to four more types of angles today: corresponding, alternate interior, alternate exterior, and consecutive interior. Begin by showing the students a transparency of two parallel lines crossed by a transversal; make sure the lines are all drawn thick and dark. This is obviously easier to do if you have an overhead projector, but it also works without one. Now cut the transparency in half, right between the parallel lines. Stack the halves on top of each other, lining up the corresponding angles. Pick any angle and show that there are three other angles with that same measurement. Next, remind students about supplementary angles and discuss how they could find the measure of the other four angles. Once they understand that there are four angles with one measure and four other angles measuring (180 – that number), the actual identification process begins. Using the student handout, go through each type of angle and its placement with respect to the parallel lines and the transversal. Finish off with the student worksheet.	**1.** 40° **2.** 180° **3.** 155° **4.** 40° **5.** 90° **6.** 115° **7.** 40° **8.** 90° **9.** 180° **10.** 140° **11.** 140° **12.** 65° **13.** 245°

Parallel Lines, Transversals, and the Angles They Form:
Student Handout

Name: _____ Date: _____ Hr: _____

When a pair of parallel lines is crossed by a transversal, many types of angles appear.

Parallel Lines
Lines that are in the same plane but never cross are called parallel lines.

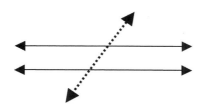

Transversal
A line that crosses two or more lines in the same plane is called a transversal.

Number the two clusters of angles that are formed when the transversal crosses the parallel lines in a clockwise manner. When you do this, all of the even-numbered angles are equal in measure and all of the odd-numbered angles are equal in measure.

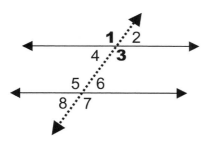

Vertical Angles
Angles across from each other when two lines cross are vertical angles. Vertical angles are equal. These are the pairs of vertical angles:

- 1 and 3   • 2 and 4
- 5 and 7   • 6 and 8

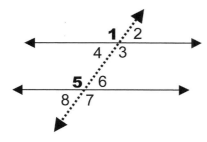

Corresponding Angles
Angles in the top cluster and in the bottom cluster that are in the same position (Ex. above the parallel line and left of the transversal) are corresponding angles. Corresponding angles are equal. These are the pairs of corresponding angles:

- 1 and 5   • 2 and 6
- 3 and 7   • 4 and 8

From *Making Math Accessible for the At-Risk Student: Grades 7–12* by Linda Ptacek. Santa Barbara, CA: Libraries Unlimited. Copyright © 2011.

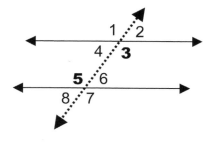

Alternate Interior Angles

A pair of angles caught inside of the parallel lines but on opposite sides of the transversal are alternate interior angles. Alternate interior angles are equal. These are the pairs of alternate interior angles:

- 4 and 6
- 3 and 5

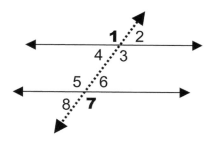

Alternate Exterior Angles

Two angles outside of the parallel lines and on opposite sides of the transversal are alternate exterior angles. Alternate exterior angles are equal. These are the pairs of alternate exterior angles:

- 1 and 7
- 2 and 8

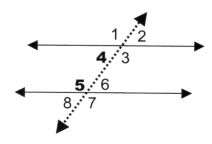

Consecutive Interior Angles

Two angles inside of the parallel lines and on the same side of the transversal are consecutive interior angles. The sum of the measures of consecutive interior angles is 180°. These are the pairs of consecutive interior angles:

- 4 and 5
- 3 and 6

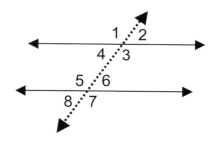

Supplementary Angles

If the sum of the measures of two angles is 180°, they are called supplementary angles. They do not need to be next to each other. Some pairs of supplementary angles are:

- 1 and 2
- 1 and 4
- 1 and 8
- 2 and 3
- 2 and 5
- 2 and 7

Any pair of angles formed when a transversal intersects two parallel lines

fits into one of the following categories.

<u>Either they are the same measure</u>   OR   <u>the sum of their measures equals 180°</u>.

Parallel Lines, Transversals, and the Angles They Form: Student Worksheet

Activity 37		
P	A	G

Name: _____ Date: _____ Hr: _____

Directions: Use the drawing below to calculate the measurements of the angles in Problems 1–13. Lines AD and BH are parallel.

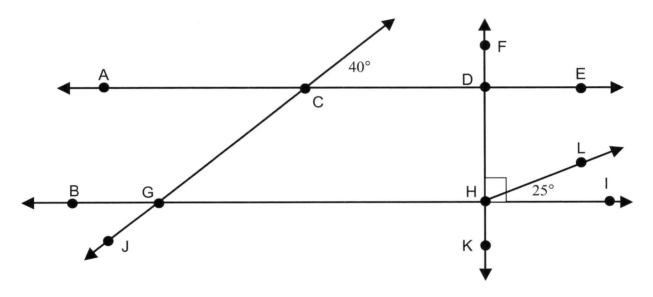

1. m∠BGJ = _____°

2. m∠BGH = _____°

3. m∠LHG = _____°

4. m∠ACG = _____°

5. m∠FDC = _____°

6. m∠LHK = _____°

7. m∠CGH= _____°

8. m∠KHG = _____°

9. m∠FDK = _____°

10. m∠BGC = _____°

11. m∠DCG = _____°

12. m∠ DHL = _____°

13. m∠LHK (reflex angle) = _____°

GAME

Pass It On: Teacher Page

Content: Review game

Standard(s):

Quick view: Pass It On is a "row race" game where students pass a game sheet backwards through their row, with each person choosing a problem to complete and then passing the sheet on. Students should be comfortable with the material before playing the game. This is NOT an introductory activity. Activity 38 focuses on plotting ordered pairs and is for pre-algebra. In Activity 39 students are asked to sketch geometric figures.

The set-up: Make one copy of the game sheet for each row of students in your classroom. If necessary, move students around to make the rows as even as possible. This works best with rows of four or five students because it reduces wait time as others in the row finish their problems.

The play: Explain the game to the students, then give the first person in each row a game sheet. When you say "GO" the first person quickly selects one of the problems, completes it, and then passes the sheet back to the next person. The last person in the row brings the game sheet back to the front person. Continue until all problems are completed. The winner is the row with the most problems correct.

Solutions for the geometry game are on the page following the game board. Solutions for problems 11–20 of the pre-algebra game are listed below. For scoring the actual point-plotting segment of the game, it will be easiest to plot the points yourself on the game sheet.

11. P	**12.** T	**13.** Q	**14.** M	**15.** S
16. R	**17.** N	**18.** L	**19.** K	**20.** V

GAME

Pass It On: Plotting Ordered Pairs

Name: _____ Date: _____ Hr: _____

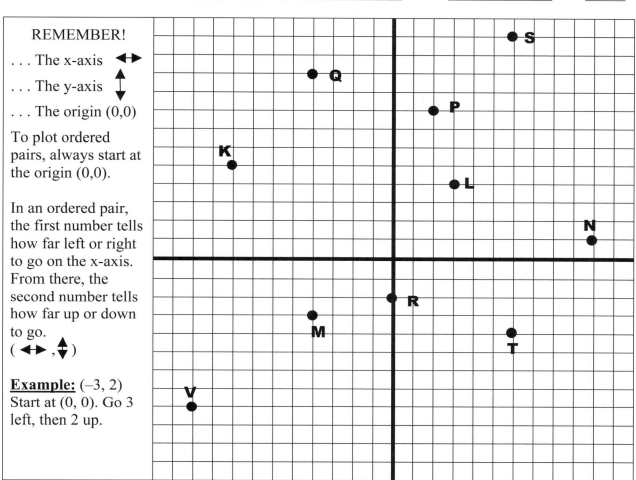

REMEMBER!

. . . The x-axis

. . . The y-axis

. . . The origin (0,0)

To plot ordered pairs, always start at the origin (0,0).

In an ordered pair, the first number tells how far left or right to go on the x-axis. From there, the second number tells how far up or down to go. (,)

Example: (–3, 2) Start at (0, 0). Go 3 left, then 2 up.

Plot these ordered pairs above and label them with the letter.		**Which letter above represents each of these ordered pairs?**	
1. (8, 0) A	**6.** (8, –2) F	**11.** (2, 8) _____	**16.** (0, –2) _____
2. (9, –12) B	**7.** (0, 5) G	**12.** (6, –4) _____	**17.** (10, 1) _____
3. (4, –3) C	**8.** (–3, 5) H	**13.** (–4, 10) _____	**18.** (3, 4) _____
4. (1, –11) D	**9.** (–6, –5) I	**14.** (–4, –3) _____	**19.** (–8, 5) _____
5. (7, 3) E	**10.** (2, –6) J	**15.** (6, 12) _____	**20.** (–10, –8) _____

GAME

Pass It On: Geometric Shapes: Student Game Board

Activity 39	
P	
A	
G	

Name: _____ Date: _____ Hr: _____

Acute angle	Supplementary angles	Transversal	Angle	Line	Vertex
Hexagon	Point	Parallel lines	Trapezoid	Chord	Tangent
Equilateral triangle	Radius	Complementary angles	Diameter	Parallelogram	Perimeter
Vertical angles	Straight angle	Line segment	Scalene triangle	Obtuse triangle	Area
Ray	Isosceles triangle	Right angle	Right angle	Adjacent angles	Circumference
Rhombus	Pentagon	3.14	Collinear points	Arc	Obtuse angle

GAME

Pass It On: Geometric Shapes: KEY

Activity 39		
P	A	G

Acute angle	**Supplementary angles**	**Transversal**	**Angle**	**Line**	**Vertex**
Hexagon	**Point**	**Parallel lines**	**Trapezoid**	**Chord**	**Tangent**
Equilateral triangle	**Radius**	**Complementary angles**	**Diameter**	**Parallelogram**	**Perimeter**
Vertical angles	**Straight angle**	**Line segment**	**Scalene triangle**	**Obtuse triangle**	**Area**
Ray	**Isosceles triangle**	**Right angle**	**Perpendicular lines**	**Adjacent angles**	**Circumference**
Rhombus	**Pentagon**	**3.14** π	**Collinear points**	**Arc**	**Obtuse angle**

From *Making Math Accessible for the At-Risk Student: Grades 7–12* by Linda Ptacek. Santa Barbara, CA: Libraries Unlimited. Copyright © 2011.

127

LESSON

Prime Factorization, Check-Double-Check: Teacher Page

Content: Prime factorization using two methods

Activity 40		
P	**A**	G

Standard(s):

About This Activity (Introducing the Methods) . . .

This check-double-check activity, designed for partners, practices two different methods for finding the prime factorization of numbers: **factor trees** and the **divide-down** method. Before you begin this activity, quickly review the terms *prime* and *factor,* along with basic *divisibility rules*. Next, demonstrate the two methods shown below, working several examples each way.

The Factor Tree	**The Divide-Down Method**
is a good method for students who have a solid command of their multiplication facts and divisibility rules. It allows them to start with any pair of factors. The randomness of this method sometimes bothers students with disabilities. If so, they might prefer the more sequential "divide-down" method shown to the right.	is a good method for students who do not know all of their facts and rules but who <u>can</u> divide using a list of prime numbers. Have students list the first eight prime numbers on the side of their paper before they start. Begin by "dividing down" by the first prime number if possible. Use it for as many layers as you can, then move on to the next prime, and continue until your answer is a prime.

The Factor Tree:

36
↙ ↘
3   12
  ↙ ↘
 2   6
   ↙ ↘
  2   3

$36 = 3 \times 2 \times 2 \times 3$
$= 2^2 \times 3^2$

The Divide-Down Method:

2 | 36
2 | 18
3 | 9
    3

$36 = 2 \times 2 \times 3 \times 3$
$= 2^2 \times 3^2$

Primes
2
3
5
7
11
13
17
19

For the worksheet . . .

Pair up students and assign each partner a letter (X or Y). "X" students do problems 1–8 with the **factor tree** method and problems 9–16 with the **divide-down** method. Reverse the methods for the "Y" students. When they have finished the problems, they should compare answers and rework any problems where their answers are not the same. When everyone has finished, have a brief discussion with the students about which method they prefer and why. Since the focus of this activity is the comparison of the methods, the numbers to be factored are relatively small.

Three advantages of this type of activity for at-risk students are:

- Students receive immediate feedback about their answers.

- By introducing two different methods, students are offered an alternative tool.

- It provides an opportunity for peer interaction that is not graded, timed, or pressured.

Solutions

1. $2^2 \times 3^2 \times 5$
2. $3 \times 5 \times 23$
3. $2^4 \times 11$
4. 7^3
5. $2^2 \times 3 \times 7$
6. $2^2 \times 5 \times 13$
7. $2 \times 5 \times 23$
8. $3 \times 5 \times 11$
9. $2 \times 7 \times 13$
10. $2^3 \times 3^2$
11. $2^2 \times 3^3$
12. $2^5 \times 3$
13. $2^3 \times 7$
14. $3^3 \times 11$
15. $2 \times 3^3 \times 7$
16. $2^2 \times 7^2$

LESSON

Prime Factorization, Check-Double-Check: Student Worksheet

Name: _____ Date: _____ Hr: _____

Set 1: The teacher will assign the method you should use.

1. 180	**2.** 345	**3.** 176	**4.** 343
5. 84	**6.** 260	**7.** 230	**8.** 165

Set 2: The teacher will assign the method you should use.

9. 182	10. 72	11. 108	12. 96
13. 56	14. 297	15. 378	16. 196

When you have finished and compared answers, discuss this question with your partner:
Which method do you like best? Why?

REVIEW

Properties of Real Numbers: Teacher Page

Content: Properties of real numbers

Standard(s):

About This Activity . . .

Many students with disabilities have difficulty remembering the properties of real numbers.
This review packet is designed for those students. It looks at the properties from three
perspectives: numeric, algebraic, and real-world examples. Develop a set of hints to help them
remember as many of the properties as you can. For example, you can remember the
COmmutative Property by noting that the CO stands for "change order." Having the students
act out the properties with 8 ½ × 11 sized signs is another fun way to see the properties in
action. Finally, it is always helpful to have the students make flash cards with the properties on
the front and a numeric example on the back and practice them for five minutes in class each
day. Count it as your warm-up activity. Students can also pair up and use two sets of flash
cards. One set is placed on the desks "property up," and the other set is placed "example up."
That way it becomes a giant matching game that students will enjoy more than practicing
alone.

Solutions to the Student Worksheet

1. G **2.** I **3.** F **4.** E **5.** H **6.** A **7.** D **8.** B **9.** C

Name: _____ Date: _____ Hr: _____

COMMUTATIVE Property of Addition
The order in which numbers are added does not change their sum.

Numbers	$61 + 5 = 5 + 61$
Algebra	$a + b = b + a$
Real-Life Example	If you eat 6 cookies and then 3 more, that is the same as eating 3 cookies, and then 6 more. Both equal 9 cookies. $6 + 3 = 3 + 6$
Your Turn➔	According to the commutative property of addition, $x + 7 = $ _____ + _____

COMMUTATIVE Property of Multiplication
The order in which numbers are multiplied does not change their product.

Numbers	$12 \times 5 = 5 \times 12$
Algebra	$a \bullet b = b \bullet a$
Real-Life Example	Sam worked 4 hours a day for 8 days = Jake worked 8 hours a day for 4 days. $4 \times 8 = 32$ and $8 \times 4 = 32$
Your Turn➔	According to the commutative property of multiplication, $a \bullet 3 = $ _____ $\bullet$ _____

ASSOCIATIVE Property of Addition
The grouping of numbers when adding does not change their sum.

Numbers	$(2 + 3) + 4 = 2 + (3 + 4)$
Algebra	$(a + b) + c = a + (b + c)$
Real-Life Example	Joe, Bobby, and George are all in Joe's dad's car. No matter who is in the back and who is in the front, there are still three boys in the car. (Joe + Bobby) + George = Joe + (Bobby + George)
Your Turn➔	According to the associative property of addition, $(x + y) + z = $ _____ + (_____ + _____)

ASSOCIATIVE Property of Multiplication
The grouping of numbers when multiplying does not change their product.

Numbers	$(5 \cdot 6) \cdot 7 = 5 \cdot (6 \cdot 7)$
Algebra	$(a \cdot b) \cdot c = a \cdot (b \cdot c)$
Real-Life Example	(\$8 per hour × 20 hours per week) × 4 weeks per month = \$640 \$8 per hour × (20 hours per week × 4 weeks per month) = \$640
Your Turn➔	According to the associative property of addition, $(2 \cdot 3) \cdot 4 = \underline{\quad} \cdot (\underline{\quad} \cdot \underline{\quad})$

DISTRIBUTIVE Property
Multiply across the parentheses. Each element inside the parentheses is multiplied by the letter or number outside of the parentheses.

Numbers	$3 \cdot (4 + 5) = 3 \cdot 4 + 3 \cdot 5$
Algebra	$a \cdot (b + c) = a \cdot b + a \cdot c$
Real-Life Example	Annie and Beth go trick-or-treating. At the first house someone says, "Oh, here are 6 pieces of candy for you to split." At the second house someone hands each girl 3 pieces of candy. 3 (Annie + Beth) = 3 Annie + 3 Beth
Your Turn➔	According to the distributive property, $4 (x + 2) = \underline{\quad} \cdot \underline{\quad} + \underline{\quad} \cdot \underline{\quad}$

ADDITIVE IDENTITY Property
Adding zero to anything does not change its identity.

Numbers	$13 + 0 = 13$
Algebra	$b + 0 = b$
Real-Life Example	Jodi read 20 pages of her book yesterday and 0 pages today. She is still on page page 20. 20 + 0 = 20
Your Turn➔	According to the additive identity property, $42 + \underline{\quad} = 42$

MULTIPLICATIVE IDENTITY Property
Multiplying anything by 1 does not change its identity.

Numbers	$12 \times 1 = 12$
Algebra	$b \times 1 = b$
Real-Life Example	Julie earns \$10 per hour tutoring. She worked 1 hour and earned \$10. $10 \times 1 = 10$
Your Turn→	According to the multiplicative identity property, $7 \times$ _____ $= 7$

ADDITIVE INVERSE Property
Adding a number and its opposite equals zero.

Numbers	$23 + (-23) = 0$
Algebra	$b + (-b) = 0$
Real-Life Example	Jerry earned \$75 mowing lawns yesterday. Then he lost his wallet with the \$75 in it. He has \$0 left. $75 + (-75) = 0$
Your Turn→	According to the additive inverse property, $14 +$ _____ $= 0$

MULTIPLICATIVE INVERSE Property
Multiplying a number by its reciprocal equals 1.

Numbers	$\dfrac{2}{7} \times \dfrac{7}{2} = 1$
Algebra	$b \times \dfrac{1}{b} = 1$
Real-Life Example	Twelve children shared a dozen donuts. Each one got $\dfrac{1}{12}$ of them, or 1 donut. $12 \times \dfrac{1}{12} = 1$
Your Turn→	According to the multiplicative inverse property, $\dfrac{3}{4} \times$ _____ $= 1$

Properties of Real Numbers

Name: _____ Date: _____ Hr: _____

Practice Problems

Match the property names in the left column with their examples in the right column.

1. _____   Additive Identity Property   **A.** $9 \times 3 = 3 \times 9$

2. _____   Additive Inverse Property   **B.** $k \times 1 = k$

3. _____   Associative Property of Addition   **C.** $\dfrac{5}{8} \times \dfrac{8}{5} = 1$

4. _____   Associative Property of Multiplication   **D.** $7(x + y) = 7x + 7y$

5. _____   Commutative Property of Addition   **E.** $(5 \times 6) \times 7 = 5 \times (6 \times 7)$

6. _____   Commutative Property of Multiplication   **F.** $(w + x) + y = w + (x + y)$

7. _____   Distributive Property   **G.** $b + 0 = b$

8. _____   Multiplicative Identity Property   **H.** $m + k = k + m$

9. _____   Multiplicative Inverse Property   **I.** $v + (-v) = 0$

GAME

Quads: Teacher Page

Content: Linear equations in slope-intercept and standard form

Standard(s):

The set-up: Prior to class, cut up enough scrap paper ($\frac{1}{4}$ sheets) so that each team has 20 answer pages. Also before class, decide on teams of four and name each team with a letter of the alphabet. Choose a reliable student to be the "chaser" and not on a team. That person will collect the teams' answers during the game and record points for correct answers. At the beginning of class, assign the teams to different parts of the classroom and ask them to cluster their desks facing each other in a huddle. Ask each group to select a recorder who will write the team's answers on their answer sheets and submit them. Give each recorder that team's scrap paper and ask her to write their team letter on each of the papers. Write the teams' alphabet letters on the board; the chaser will record points there. Explain the game to the class and remind them to keep their voices low so that the other teams do not overhear their answers.

The play: The teacher will read a math question. Teams will decide on their answer and write it on a scrap paper, then fold it in half. After a reasonable amount of time, the teacher will call "UP," and each team's recorder will raise the team's answer to be collected by the chaser. After the chaser has collected all of the answer sheets, the teacher will announce the correct solution. The chaser will then record points for correct team answers on the board. The winner is the quad with the most points. In the event that a tie-breaker is needed, ask one more question, and the first team with the correct answer wins.

GAME	Activity 42		
Quads: Equations and Solutions: Teacher Page	**P**	**A**	**G**

1. Put into slope-intercept form: $2x + y = 9$.	**1.** $y = -2x + 9$
2. Put into slope-intercept form: $y - 5x = 20$.	**2.** $y = 5x + 20$
3. Put into slope-intercept form: $3x = y + 24$.	**3.** $y = 3x - 24$
4. Put into slope-intercept form: $-2x + y = 14$.	**4.** $y = 2x + 14$
5. Put into slope-intercept form: $3x + y = 12$.	**5.** $y = -3x + 12$
6. Put into slope-intercept form: $-9x + 3y = -6$.	**6.** $y = 3x - 2$
7. Put into slope-intercept form: $4x + 2y = -20$.	**7.** $y = -2x - 10$
8. Write the equation of a line with a slope of 8 and y-intercept of -2.	**8.** $y = 8x - 2$
9. Write the equation of a line with a slope of 7 and y-intercept of 6.	**9.** $y = 7x + 6$
10. Write the equation of a line with a slope of 4 and y-intercept of 2.	**10.** $y = 4x + 2$
11. Write the equation of a line with a -5 slope and y-intercept of -8.	**11.** $y = -5x - 8$
12. Find the x-intercept and y-intercept: $3x + 2y = -12$.	**12.** $(0, -6)\ (-4, 0)$
13. Find the x-intercept and y-intercept: $-5x - 10y = 20$.	**13.** $(0, -2)\ (-4, 0)$
14. Find the x-intercept and y-intercept: $x - 8y = 16$.	**14.** $(0, -2)\ (16, 0)$
15. Find the x-intercept and y-intercept: $9x - 4y = -36$.	**15.** $(0, 9)\ (-4, 0)$
16. Find the x-intercept and y-intercept: $8x + 5y = 40$.	**16.** $(0, 8)\ (5, 0)$
17. Put into standard form: $y = -2x + 8$.	**17.** $2x + y = 8$
18. Put into standard form: $y = 3x - 15$.	**18.** $3x - y = 15$
19. Put into standard form: $2x = -5y + 10$.	**19.** $2x + 5y = 10$
20. Put into standard form: $2x + 12 = 3y$.	**20.** $2x - 3y = -12$

RAP (Review-and-Practice) Cards: Teacher Page

	Activity 43	
P	**A**	**G**

Content: Review format for any content

About This Activity . . .

RAP cards are laminated worksheets placed in folders on the bulletin board that students can do for bonus points when they have extra time. See the illustration below. Remind students not to remove the cards from the classroom! For each quarter, outline a set of 5 to 10 skills you would like to have the students review from the <u>previous</u> quarter. Write the concept names in large letters on the front of file folders and staple them like pockets to the bulletin board. Next, find one worksheet for each concept that has a quick and easy-to-follow review at the top of the page. Determine the mastery level a student must achieve in order to earn the bonus points, and indicate that on the board if it will be the same for all activities or on the card if it will vary from card to card. Laminate the worksheets and put them into the appropriate folders. For organization purposes, label the folders and their worksheets with the same letters (see diagram). As students finish their assignments, they can go to the bulletin board and find a RAP card to complete. They can write on them with an overhead pen. After a student finishes a card, it is easy to wipe off and return to its folder. Remember to devise a system to keep track of which cards students have done, so they do not accidentally do the same card twice. A sign-in notebook or 3 x 5 card file system is fairly simple. The sign-in sheet could be formatted like the one below.

RAP Cards Completed

Student Name	Date	Folder/Card Letter	Mastery Y/N

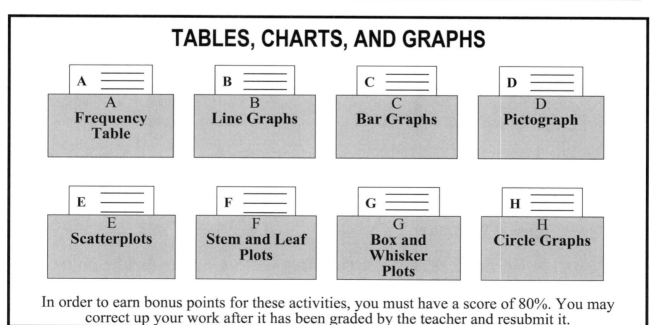

TABLES, CHARTS, AND GRAPHS

A	B	C	D
A Frequency Table	**B** Line Graphs	**C** Bar Graphs	**D** Pictograph

E	F	G	H
E Scatterplots	**F** Stem and Leaf Plots	**G** Box and Whisker Plots	**H** Circle Graphs

In order to earn bonus points for these activities, you must have a score of 80%. You may correct up your work after it has been graded by the teacher and resubmit it.

LESSON

The Real Number System, No Leftovers: Teacher Page

Content: Real numbers

Standard(s):

	Activity 44	
P	A	G

About This Activity . . .

Gather a set of four nesting food-storage containers. Find a fifth container similar in size but with a different shape. Finally, find a box that all of the containers will fit into. Label the nesting containers smallest to largest: NATURAL, WHOLE, INTEGER, and RATIONAL. The different-shaped container is IRRATIONAL, and the box is REAL. Cut two or three shapes from poster board that fit <u>exactly</u> inside each of the plastic containers, and on them write numbers that belong to that set. Before the students come into class, tape all of the number tags onto the board. At the start of class, tell the students that you will be introducing the real number system today. Explain that in the real number system, there are no leftovers: Every number fits into a category (show containers). One-by-one, have volunteers go to the board, take a number tag, and put it into the appropriate-sized container. When all of the tags are gone, nest the containers and discuss how numbers that fit into the smallest set also fit into the larger ones but not vice versa. Give each student the accompanying diagram of the real number system and ask them to save it as a reference. After a short discussion of the number system and additional practice numbers, pass out the **Number Tag** song (see Activity 32) and sing it as a group to reinforce the content. Finally, complete the student worksheet.

Solutions to Student Worksheet

1. NA, WH, IN, RA, RE **2.** IR, RE **3.** RA, RE **4.** RA, RE **5.** RA, RE **6.** WH, IN, RA, RE

7. RA, RE **8.** IR, RE **9.** RA, RE **10.** RA, RE **11.** RA, RE **12.** IN, RA, RE

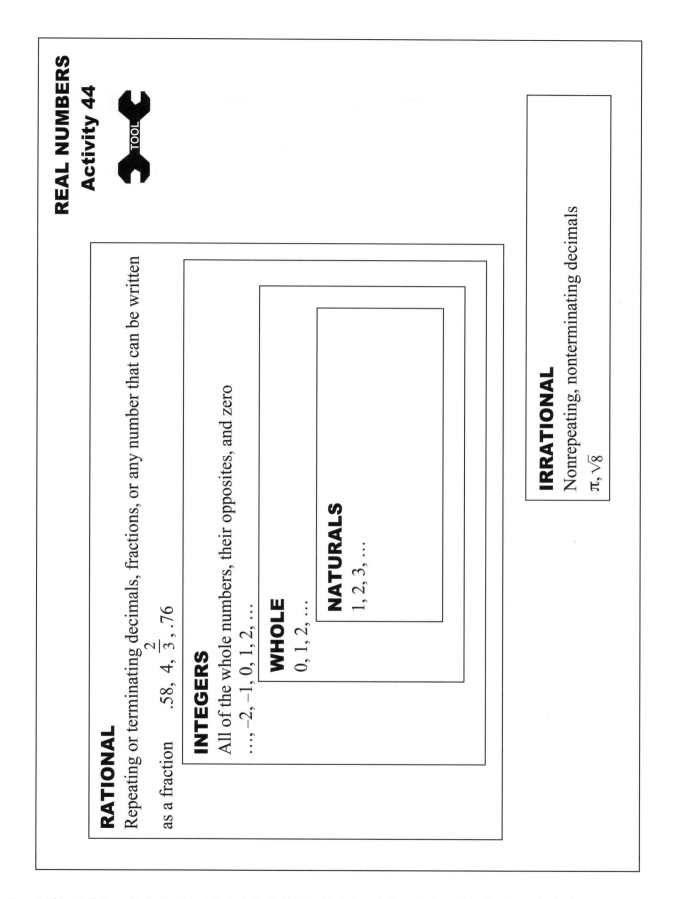

RATIONAL
Repeating or terminating decimals, fractions, or any number that can be written

as a fraction $.58, \ 4, \ \frac{2}{3}, \ .76$

INTEGERS
All of the whole numbers, their opposites, and zero
$\dots, -2, -1, 0, 1, 2, \dots$

WHOLE
$0, 1, 2, \dots$

NATURALS
$1, 2, 3, \dots$

IRRATIONAL
Nonrepeating, nonterminating decimals
$\pi, \sqrt{8}$

The Real Number System, No Leftovers: Student Worksheet

	Activity 44	
P	**A**	**G**

Name: _____ Date: _____ Hr: _____

Directions: Examine the numbers below and put an x in each category to which they belong:

NA (Natural)   **WH** (Whole)   **IN** (Integer)   **RA** (Rational)   **IR** (Irrational)   **RE** (Real)

		NA	WH	IN	RA	IR	RE
1.	7						
2.	$\sqrt{8}$						
3.	.14						
4.	$2.\overline{23}$						
5.	$-\dfrac{8}{9}$						
6.	0						
7.	7.19						
8.	Pi						
9.	38%						
10.	$\dfrac{1}{3}$						
11.	$\dfrac{9}{4}$						
12.	−73						

LESSON

Varsity Sue, a Readers Theater Play: Teacher Page

Content: Circle terminology

Standard(s):

About This Activity . . .

This activity is designed as a small group activity for special education students who are working significantly below grade level and must have their work modified. The readability level of the play is 2.9. It can also be used with English language learner students who have limited English proficiency. Run one copy of the play for each student.

Objectives:

- The student will improve reading fluency and comprehension in a curricular area.

- The student will draw and define the center, radius, diameter, and semicircle.

- The student will use a string, pencil, and thumbtack to construct a 10 inch circle.

Prereading activity:

- List the following geometry terms side-by-side across the board: **circle, radius, diameter, compass, semicircle, arc, center.**

- Tell the students that each of these terms appears in the reading that follows. Ask for student volunteers to define them (in their own words) and to sketch them (underneath the word on the board.)

- Assign readers for each role: Mom, Dad, Sue, and Narrator.

Postreading activity:

- Review the vocabulary.

- Model the string trick for the students, then have students work in pairs to make circles on poster board. Each pair should make two circles, one for each partner.

- On each completed circle, draw and label the center, radius, diameter, arc, and then shade in one semicircle.

Varsity Sue, a Readers Theater Play

Name: _____ Date: _____ Hr: _____

Characters: Narrator, Dad, Mom, Sue

Narrator: It is Friday afternoon and girls' basketball tryouts have been going on all week. Today the teams were announced. Sue, a high school freshman, has just returned home from school in a very good mood.

Dad: Well, I guess from the smile on your face, congratulations are in order for you, Sue. Which team did you make, Varsity, JV, or ninth grade?

Sue: Varsity, Dad! I was pretty worried for a while. Fifty girls tried out and a lot of them were really good.

Mom: Maybe we should do something special to celebrate. What do you think, Sue? A movie? Pizza? Any ideas?

Sue: What I would really like to do is to fix up my room, Mom.

Mom: Clean your room? I can't argue with that plan, but it doesn't sound like much of a celebration to me.

Sue: Not clean my room, Mom. Fix it up. You know, decorate it.

Mom: What did you have in mind?

Sue: Well, since I made the team, I wanted to use a basketball theme. I thought a round basketball mirror and a basketball headboard would be fun.

Mom: Well, we have been talking about repainting your room anyway. This might be a perfect time to paint <u>and</u> redecorate.

Dad: I even have some wood in the garage that we could use to make the headboard and mirror backing.

Sue: Can I help?

Dad: I was hoping you would offer. Let's go take a few measurements before we get started. You know what they say, "Measure twice; cut once!"

Narrator: Sue and her dad head off to her room to measure the width of her bed and to decide just how big a mirror she wants. When they have finished, they go out to the garage to start their project.

Dad: Well, we have our wood, the paint, and the measurements. Our biggest problem, as far as I can see, is how to cut out a perfect **circle** that is so large.

Sue: I think I can help with that, Dad. We learned a simple trick in math class this year using a string and a pencil.

Dad: Really? Tell me about it.

Sue: Well, if we want to do a three-foot circle to glue the mirror on, first we figure out how far halfway across the circle would be. Three feet is 36 inches, so half of that would be 18 inches.

Dad: That is the circle's **radius**, right? From the center of the circle out to the edge?

Sue: Right, Dad. The 36-inch measurement, all the way across, is the **diameter**.

Dad: I knew that! Your old dad was pretty good at math too!

Sue: But you never used the string trick?

Dad: Nope. I always used a **compass** to make circles. Until today, I never really needed to make a circle that was too big to use a compass. Keep explaining the string trick to me, and I will follow your directions.

Sue: Well, you can make your own jumbo compass for big projects using a string and a pencil. First, cut a piece of string two inches longer than the radius of the circle you want to draw. Tie one end of the string around a pencil near the point. Tie the other end around a tack or small nail.

Dad: OK. The string is cut and tied. Now what?

Sue: Push the tack into the board where you want the center of the circle to be.

From *Making Math Accessible for the At-Risk Student: Grades 7–12* by Linda Ptacek. Santa Barbara, CA: Libraries Unlimited. Copyright © 2011.

Dad: Got it. I'm ready for the next step.

Sue: Now all you have to do is pull the string really tight and move the pencil around in a big **arc**.

Narrator: Dad follows Sue's directions, making a perfect circle.

Dad: What do you think of my circle, Sue? Not bad for a first try, even if I do say so myself!

Sue: It looks great, Dad. Let's go ahead and draw out the headboard next. This time we only need a **semicircle** though.

Narrator: Sue and her dad refer back to the bed's measurements, and Sue starts marking the semicircle for the headboard.

Dad: Hey, you're pretty good at this too, Sue.

Sue: Thanks, Dad. Now since I taught you the string and pencil trick, will you teach me how to use your jigsaw to cut the circle out?

Dad: That seems only fair to me. Here, put on these safety goggles and let's get started!

REVIEW

What's the Difference? Teacher Page

P	A	G

Content: Semester-end review of vocabulary by finding out how concepts are different

Standard(s):

About This Activity . . .

There is so much vocabulary in math, that by the end of the semester, students' heads are swimming with words. They know that there are relationships between the words, and they can usually tell you the topic to which they relate. They might even be able to match the term and its definition. To take that learning to another level, ask them to contrast a term with another term that is in some way similar. Activity 46 focuses on pre-algebra vocabulary while Activity 47 deals with algebra vocabulary. Students are given two terms like *coefficient* and *variable* and asked, "What's the difference?" Encourage them to describe the difference in words, not examples. It is too easy to put down the first number that pops into their heads as an example, and the thinking skills stop there. Split the class into pairs and give each group three pairs of terms to contrast. When students have completed the activity, spend class time discussing each pair of words. That is the appropriate time to give examples; you might ask for several examples of each term. As a follow-up, give the students a copy of the key to review and use the terms in a game the next day. See **Cubes** (Activity 3) or **Quads** (Activity 42).

You can shorten or lengthen the activity as necessary for your group. The format works well at any level of math instruction. For those students working well below grade level, whose work is routinely modified, mark the "need-to-know" items with an asterisk. Have them focus on those terms only.

What's the Difference? Student Worksheet

Name: _____ Date: _____ Hr: _____

Directions: On your own paper, briefly tell how each pair of words is different.

1.	Additive inverse	Reciprocal
2.	Area	Volume
3.	Associative Property	Commutative Property
4.	Circumference	Perimeter
5.	Composite number	Prime number
6.	Constant	Variable
7.	Coordinate axis	Number line
8.	Denominator	Numerator
9.	Estimate	Solution
10.	Factor (Name the factors of 10.)	Multiple (Give three multiples of 10.)
11.	Finite	Infinite
12.	Improper fraction	Mixed number
13.	Integer	Whole number
14.	Like terms	Unlike terms
15.	Mean	Median
16.	Mode	Range
17.	Negative number on a number line	Positive number on a number line
18.	The first step for $(3 + 4) \times 5$	The first step for $3 + 4 \times 5$
19.	Ordered pair	Origin
20.	Parallel lines	Perpendicular lines
21.	Product	Quotient
22.	Proportion	Ratio
23.	Quadrant	Quadrilateral
24.	x-axis	y-axis
25.	x-coordinate	y-coordinate

REVIEW

What's the Difference? KEY

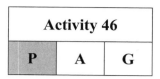

1.	**Additive inverse:** *Same number with opposite sign*	**Reciprocal:** *A fraction flipped upside down*
2.	**Area:** *The amount of space covered by a two-dimensional figure*	**Volume:** *The capacity of a filled three-dimensional figure*
3.	**Associative Property:** *Has to do with the grouping of numbers*	**Commutative Property:** *Has to do with the order of numbers*
4.	**Circumference:** *Distance around a circle*	**Perimeter:** *Distance around a polygon*
5.	**Composite number:** *A number with three or more factors*	**Prime number:** *Has only two factors, 1 and itself*
6.	**Constant:** *A number that will not change*	**Variable:** *A letter representing a number that may change*
7.	**Coordinate axis:** *Two-dimensional grid used to plot ordered pairs and lines*	**Number line:** *Horizontal line where all numbers are represented as points*
8.	**Denominator:** *Bottom number of a fraction*	**Numerator:** *Top number of a fraction*
9.	**Estimate:** *A number close to the answer*	**Solution:** *An exact answer*
10.	**Factors of 10:** *1, 2, 5, 10*	**Multiples of 10:** *10, 20, 30, ...*
11.	**Finite:** *Having an ending or limits*	**Infinite:** *Having no end*
12.	**Improper fraction:** *A fraction with a larger numerator than denominator*	**Mixed number:** *A number with an integer part and a fraction part*
13.	**Integer:** *. . . , –2, –1, 0, 1, 2, . . .*	**Whole number:** *0, 1, 2, . . .*

14.	**Like terms:**	**Unlike terms:**
	Terms with the same variables to the same powers	*Terms not having the same variables to the same powers*
15.	**Mean:**	**Median:**
	The average of a group of numbers	*The middle number when a group of numbers is arranged smallest to largest*
16.	**Mode:**	**Range:**
	The number(s) seen most often in a list of numbers	*The difference between the largest and smallest numbers in a group*
17.	**Negative number on a number line:**	**Positive number on a number line:**
	Located to the left of zero	*Located to the right of zero*
18.	**The first step for $(3 + 4) \times 5$**	**The first step for $3 + 4 \times 5$**
	Do $(3 + 4)$	*Multiply 4×5*
19.	**Ordered pair:**	**Origin:**
	Gives the location of any point on the coordinate axis (,)	*(0,0) on a coordinate axis*
20.	**Parallel lines:**	**Perpendicular lines:**
	Two lines in the same plane that never touch	*Two lines that intersect in a 90° angle*
21.	**Product:**	**Quotient:**
	Multiplication answer	*Division answer*
22.	**Proportion:**	**Ratio:**
	An equation that puts two ratios equal to each other	*A comparison of two numbers written in fraction form*
23.	**Quadrant:**	**Quadrilateral:**
	Section of a coordinate grid	*A four-sided polygon*
24.	**x-axis:**	**y-axis:**
	Horizontal axis on coordinate grid	*Vertical axis on coordinate grid*
25.	**x-coordinate:**	**y-coordinate:**
	First number in an ordered pair: (4, 3)	*Second number in an ordered pair: (3,4)*

What's the Difference? Student Worksheet

Name: _____ Date: _____ Hr: _____

Directions: On your own paper, briefly tell how each pair of words is different.

1.	0 divided by 5	5 divided by 0
2.	0^3	3^0
3.	Absolute value	Negative number
4.	Binomial	Trinomial
5.	Coefficient	Exponent
6.	Composite number	Prime number
7.	Constant	Variable
8.	Cubed	Squared
9.	Domain	Range
10.	Equation	Expression
11.	Factor (List the factors of 10.)	Multiple (Give three multiples of 10.)
12.	Factoring quadratic trinomials	Prime factorization
13.	Finite	Infinite
14.	Integers	Rational numbers
15.	Like terms	Unlike terms
16.	Negative slope	Positive slope
17.	Rise	Run
18.	Slope of a horizontal line	Slope of a vertical line
19.	Slope of parallel lines	Slope of perpendicular lines
20.	The graph of $x > 4$	The graph of $x \geq 4$

What's the Difference? KEY

1.	**0 divided by 5:** *0*	**5 divided by 0:** *Undefined*
2.	**0^3:** *0*	**3^0:** *Anything to the zero power = 1*
3.	**Absolute value:** *Distance from 0 on number line; always positive*	**Negative number:** *Left of 0 on number line*
4.	**Binomial:** *Expression with two terms*	**Trinomial:** *Expression with three terms*
5.	**Coefficient:** *Number in front of a variable*	**Exponent:** *A number showing how many times something is multiplied by itself*
6.	**Composite number:** *Has three or more factors*	**Prime number:** *Only two factors, 1 and itself*
7.	**Constant:** *A number that will not change*	**Variable:** *Letter representing a number*
8.	**Cubed:** *Multiplied by itself three times*	**Squared:** *Multiplied by itself twice*
9.	**Domain:** *Possible x-values in a function*	**Range:** *Possible y-values in a function*
10.	**Equation:** *A statement that two expressions are equal*	**Expression:** *Combination of variables, numbers, and operation symbols*
11.	**Factors of 10:** *1, 2, 5, 10*	**Multiples of 10:** *10, 20, 30, ...*
12.	**Factoring quadratic trinomials:** *Breaking them down into their binomial factors*	**Prime factorization:** *A number broken down to the product of its prime factors*
13.	**Finite:** *Has an ending or limits*	**Infinite:** *Has no ending or limits*
14.	**Integers:** *Positive and negative whole numbers and zero*	**Rational numbers:** *Any number that can be expressed in fraction form*
15.	**Like terms:** *Terms having the same variables to the same powers*	**Unlike terms:** *Terms that do not have the same variables to the same powers*
16.	**Negative slope:**	**Positive slope:**
17.	**Rise:** *Change in y-value on a graphed line*	**Run:** *Change in x-value on a graphed line*
18.	**Slope of a horizontal line:** *Zero*	**Slope of a vertical line:** *Undefined*
19.	**Slope of parallel lines:** *Equal*	**Slope of perpendicular lines:** *Reciprocals with opposite signs*
20.	**The graph of x > 4:**	**The graph of x ≥ 4:**

REVIEW

What's Your Angle? Teacher Page

Content: Measuring angles

Standard(s):

<table>
<tr><td>Activity 48</td></tr>
<tr><td>P</td><td>A</td><td>G</td></tr>
</table>

About This Activity . . .

If you love to take pictures in your free time, designing this bulletin board will not even seem like work! This interactive bulletin board activity is one that students can do when they have extra time at the end of class. It includes photos taken inside the school, around town, and on trips. Staple four file folders to the bulletin board as pockets and label them as in the diagram on the following page. Use 10 photos per folder, 5 in each of two small manila envelopes. Each photo should have a component that has a clearly defined angle that students can measure. Use a permanent marker to define the angles on the photos. Once again, remember to devise a system to keep track of which students have done the activity. A sample record sheet is shown below.

A fun photo option:

Ask each student in the class to pose for an "angle" shot by forming the angle of their choice with their arms.

"What's Your Angle" Record Sheet for Hour _____

Student Name	Date	Packet(s) Completed	Number Correct

What's Your Angle?

Take a protractor, a worksheet, and one packet of photos.

Return to your seat and measure the angles marked on each photo.

Record each angle's measurement next to the photo's number on the worksheet.

Return the photos and get more if you have time. For every 5 photos measured correctly, you can earn 1 bonus point on your next quiz. Save your worksheet until you have measured all the angles you plan to do, then turn it in to the teacher.

PROTRACTORS

Please remember to return your protractor to this packet.

WORKSHEETS

Please take only 1 worksheet.

| Packet A
Photos
1-5 | Packet B
Photos
6-10 | Packet C
Photos
11-15 | Packet D
Photos
16-20 | Packet E
Photos
21-25 | Packet F
Photos
26-30 |

Photos Around The School

Photos Around Town

Vacation Photos

Sample Photo: Liberty Memorial, Kansas City, Missouri

REVIEW

What's Your Angle? Student Worksheet

Name: _____ Date: _____ Hr: _____

Directions: Write the measurement of the angles for your photo cards next to the number matching the card. For every five photos measured correctly, you can earn one bonus point on your next quiz. Save your worksheet until you have measured all of the photos you plan to do, then turn it in.

Photos around the School

Packet A   **Packet B**

1 _____   6 _____

2 _____   7 _____

3 _____   8 _____

4 _____   9 _____

5 _____   10 _____

Photos around Town

Packet C   **Packet D**

11 _____   16 _____

12 _____   17 _____

13 _____   18 _____

14 _____   19 _____

15 _____   20 _____

Vacation Photos

Packet E   **Packet F**

21 _____   26 _____

22 _____   27 _____

23 _____   28 _____

24 _____   29 _____

25 _____   30 _____

What's Your First Step? Teacher Page

Content: Solving equations

Standard(s):

About This Activity . . .

This activity is intended to "jump-start" the equation-solving process. Many students seem to have difficulty getting started because they think too far ahead. For this worksheet, all they have to do is to identify their first step. The students who continually worry about not getting the right answer in the end can breathe easier for a while!

Solutions:

1. Distribute the 2. Multiply $2(x - 1)$.

2. Subtract 6 from both sides.

3. Add 4 to both sides.

4. Combine the $8x$ and the $2x$.

5. Add $4x$ to both sides OR subtract 4 from both sides.

6. Add 16 to both sides OR subtract $3w$ from both sides.

7. Combine $3x$ and $-4x$.

8. Distribute. Multiply $2(2x + 7)$

9. Divide both sides by -5.

10. Add 29 and 7.

11. Distribute. Multiply $-1(z + 6)$

12. Distribute. Multiply $-2(x + 1)$

What's Your First Step? Student Worksheet

	Activity 49	
P	A	G

Name: _____ Date: _____ Hr: _____

Directions: In the empty boxes to the right of each equation, briefly tell what your first step in solving the equations would be. DO NOT actually solve them.

1.	$2(x - 1) = 16$	
2.	$4x + 6 = 22$	
3.	$-4 - 3x = 20$	
4.	$8x + 2x = 40$	
5.	$6x + 4 = -4x + 1$	
6.	$7w - 16 = 3w$	
7.	$3x - 7 - 4x = 14$	
8.	$2(2x + 7) = 8x - 5$	
9.	$-5w = -55$	
10.	$12r = 29 + 7$	
11.	$5z - (z + 6) = 3z - 4$	
12.	$3 - 2(x + 1) = 13 + 10x$	

LESSON

Whatzit? Teacher Page

Content: Identifying basic geometric figures

Standard(s):

About This Activity . . .

This activity is a rapid-fire review of basic geometric figures. Once you establish the parameters for this activity, you can use the format for distributed practice with other materials throughout the year. First, give a copy of the student handout and the alphabetical list of terms to each student. The lists are run two to a page to save paper. Tell the class that you will be calling out numbers indicating figures on their handouts. They should find the figure and then respond with its name. It might get a little loud, but it is good excitement, and the students who do not know the figures will not be embarrassed by their silence or incorrect responses. Go through the entire chart once in order and a second time in a random fashion. Then ask each student to use the alphabetical list to identify all the figures on their papers. To simplify the process for students who have language or writing deficits, simply have them put the appropriate letter instead of writing out the names of the figures.

Solutions:

1. Chord - A
2. Perpendicular lines - L
3. Collinear points - B
4. Transversal - R
5. Ray - O
6. Equilateral triangle - E
7. Parallelogram - J

8. Vertex - T
9. Corresponding angles - C
10. Plane - M
11. Rhombus - P
12. Hexagon - F
13. Tangent - Q
14. Line segment - H

15. Trapezoid - S
16. Line - G
17. Diameter - D
18. Parallel lines - I
19. Pentagon - K
20. Radius - N

Whatzit? Student Handout

Whatzit? Terms

A.	Chord
B.	Collinear points
C.	Corresponding angles
D.	Diameter
E.	Equilateral triangle
F.	Hexagon
G.	Line
H.	Line segment
I.	Parallel lines
J.	Parallelogram
K.	Pentagon
L.	Perpendicular lines
M.	Plane
N.	Radius
O.	Ray
P.	Rhombus
Q.	Tangent
R.	Transversal
S.	Trapezoid
T.	Vertex

Whatzit? Terms

A.	Chord
B.	Collinear points
C.	Corresponding angles
D.	Diameter
E.	Equilateral triangle
F.	Hexagon
G.	Line
H.	Line segment
I.	Parallel lines
J.	Parallelogram
K.	Pentagon
L.	Perpendicular lines
M.	Plane
N.	Radius
O.	Ray
P.	Rhombus
Q.	Tangent
R.	Transversal
S.	Trapezoid
T.	Vertex

Whatzit? Student Handout

Name: _____ Date: _____ Hr: _____

1.	2.	3. A B C D	4.
5.	6.	7.	8.
9.	10. $\mathcal{P}$	11.	12.
13.	14.	15.	16.
17.	18.	19.	20.

ACTIVITY INDEX

Note: The topics listed below are referenced by their activity numbers rather than the page on which they can be found.

INDEX OF TEACHING TECHNIQUES

ABOUT THE AUTHOR

LINDA PTACEK is a recently retired classroom teacher with 35 years of experience teaching at the secondary and postsecondary levels. She received both her BA in secondary education and her MS in special education, behavior disorders, from the University of Kansas. She has a wide range of classroom experience in French, English, psychology, algebra, and special education classes. Over the years, Linda has presented seminars at the district level, as well as the state and national levels, on working with underachieving students, incorporating educational technology into the classroom, and developing classroom-management strategies for special education classrooms. Most recently, Linda has developed materials to help at-risk students succeed in high school algebra and geometry classes.